Prayers of Intercession

Following the Common Worship Lectionary

David Adam

kevin mayhew

kevin mayhew

First published in Great Britain in 2007 by Kevin Mayhew Ltd
Buxhall, Stowmarket, Suffolk IP14 3BW
Tel: +44 (0) 1449 737978 Fax: +44 (0) 1449 737834
E-mail: info@kevinmayhewltd.com

www.kevinmayhew.com

This hardback edition 2012

9 8 7 6 5 4 3 2 1 0

ISBN 978 1 84867 473 8
Catalogue No. 1501324

Cover design by Rob Mortonson
Typeset by Richard Weaver

Printed and bound in Great Britain

Contents

Foreword 9

YEAR A

ADVENT
First Sunday of Advent 12
Second Sunday of Advent 14
Third Sunday of Advent 16
Fourth Sunday of Advent 18

CHRISTMAS
Christmas Day 20
First Sunday of Christmas 22
Second Sunday of Christmas 24

EPIPHANY
The Epiphany 26
First Sunday of Epiphany: The Baptism of Christ 28
Second Sunday of Epiphany 30
Third Sunday of Epiphany 32
Fourth Sunday of Epiphany 34
The Presentation of Christ 36

ORDINARY TIME
Proper 1 38
Proper 2 40
Proper 3 42
Second Sunday before Lent 44
Sunday before Lent 46

LENT
First Sunday of Lent 48
Second Sunday of Lent 50
Third Sunday of Lent 52
Fourth Sunday of Lent: Mothering Sunday 54
Fifth Sunday of Lent 56
Palm Sunday 58

EASTER
Easter Day 60
Second Sunday of Easter 62

Third Sunday of Easter 64
Fourth Sunday of Easter 66
Fifth Sunday of Easter 68
Sixth Sunday of Easter 70
Ascension Day 72
Seventh Sunday of Easter 74
Pentecost 76

ORDINARY TIME
Trinity Sunday 78
Proper 4 80
Proper 5 82
Proper 6 84
Proper 7 86
Proper 8 88
Proper 9 90
Proper 10 92
Proper 11 94
Proper 12 96
Proper 13 98
Proper 14 100
Proper 15 102
Proper 16 104
Proper 17 106
Proper 18 108
Proper 19 110
Proper 20 112
Proper 21 114
Proper 22 116
Proper 23 118
Proper 24 120
Proper 25 122
All Saints' Day 124
Fourth Sunday before Advent 126
Third Sunday before Advent 128
Second Sunday before Advent 130
Christ the King 132

YEAR B

ADVENT
First Sunday of Advent 136
Second Sunday of Advent 138

Third Sunday of Advent	140
Fourth Sunday of Advent	142
CHRISTMAS	
Christmas Day	144
First Sunday of Christmas	146
Second Sunday of Christmas	148
EPIPHANY	
The Epiphany	150
First Sunday of Epiphany: The Baptism of Christ	152
Second Sunday of Epiphany	154
Third Sunday of Epiphany	156
Fourth Sunday of Epiphany	158
The Presentation of Christ	160
ORDINARY TIME	
Proper 1	162
Proper 2	164
Proper 3	166
Second Sunday before Lent	168
Sunday before Lent	170
LENT	
First Sunday of Lent	172
Second Sunday of Lent	174
Third Sunday of Lent	176
Fourth Sunday of Lent: Mothering Sunday	178
Fifth Sunday of Lent	180
Palm Sunday	182
EASTER	
Easter Day	184
Second Sunday of Easter	186
Third Sunday of Easter	188
Fourth Sunday of Easter	190
Fifth Sunday of Easter	192
Sixth Sunday of Easter	194
Ascension Day	196
Seventh Sunday of Easter	198
Pentecost	200
ORDINARY TIME	
Trinity Sunday	202
Proper 4	204

Proper 5 206
Proper 6 208
Proper 7 210
Proper 8 212
Proper 9 214
Proper 10 216
Proper 11 218
Proper 12 220
Proper 13 222
Proper 14 224
Proper 15 226
Proper 16 228
Proper 17 230
Proper 18 232
Proper 19 234
Proper 20 236
Proper 21 238
Proper 22 240
Proper 23 242
Proper 24 244
Proper 25 246
All Saints' Day 248
Fourth Sunday before Advent 250
Third Sunday before Advent 252
Second Sunday before Advent 254
Christ the King 256

YEAR C

ADVENT
First Sunday of Advent 260
Second Sunday of Advent 262
Third Sunday of Advent 264
Fourth Sunday of Advent 266

CHRISTMAS
Christmas Day 268
First Sunday of Christmas 270
Second Sunday of Christmas 272

EPIPHANY
The Epiphany 274
First Sunday of Epiphany: The Baptism of Christ 276

Second Sunday of Epiphany 278
Third Sunday of Epiphany 280
Fourth Sunday of Epiphany 282

ORDINARY TIME
Proper 1 284
Proper 2 286
Proper 3 288
Second Sunday before Lent 290
Sunday before Lent 292

LENT
First Sunday of Lent 294
Second Sunday of Lent 296
Third Sunday of Lent 298
Fourth Sunday of Lent: Mothering Sunday 300
Fifth Sunday of Lent 302
Palm Sunday 304

EASTER
Easter Day 306
Second Sunday of Easter 308
Third Sunday of Easter 310
Fourth Sunday of Easter 312
Fifth Sunday of Easter 314
Sixth Sunday of Easter 316
Ascension Day 318
Seventh Sunday of Easter 320
Pentecost 322

ORDINARY TIME
Trinity Sunday 324
Proper 4 326
Proper 5 328
Proper 6 330
Proper 7 332
Proper 8 334
Proper 9 336
Proper 10 338
Proper 11 340
Proper 12 342
Proper 13 344
Proper 14 346
Proper 15 348

Proper 16	350
Proper 17	352
Proper 18	354
Proper 19	356
Proper 20	358
Proper 21	360
Proper 22	362
Proper 23	364
Proper 24	366
Proper 25	368
All Saints' Day	370
Fourth Sunday before Advent	372
Third Sunday before Advent	374
Second Sunday before Advent	376
Christ the King	378

Foreword

When I was seeking to deepen my prayer life I was given a card with the following prayer of St Augustine upon it:

> 'Watch thou, dear Lord,
> with all who watch or wake or weep this night,
> give your angels charge over those who sleep.
> Tend your sick ones:
> refresh your weary ones:
> sustain your dying ones:
> calm your suffering ones:
> have pity on your distressed ones,
> and all for your mercy and love's sake.'

The words made me deeply aware that all belongs to God and he loves the whole of his creation. When you seek to draw near to the heart of God you realise that as you come towards his love you must let that love radiate from out of your life. You are called to be a channel of his love; let it pour into you and then out to others. Before any intercessions it is good to rejoice in the presence and in the love of God. As God cares for all of his creation and enfolds it in his love, so they who seek to acknowledge the love of God must express the same care and love for all. The closer we come to God the closer we come to one another. This will involve us in knowing not only the love of God but in his giving himself for the world. True intercession is costly as can be seen by the offering of Christ on the cross. Intercession is about offering our lives to God in communion with Christ for the redemption of the world.

Intercession involves us in the deepest of relationships for it involves us not only with God but with all of his creation. We are expressing our love and trust in God, our love and concern for each other and for the whole world. An easy way to begin intercession is always to approach God with someone or some concern in your heart and to know that you are both in the heart of God. Intercession continues when you leave your prayers with the awareness that God is in your heart as you approach others in love and care, knowing they are also in the heart of God.

In the coming to God in love we seek to lay our whole life before him in self-surrender. Intercession is not a shopping list of needs; it is seeking to place all before God in love and saying to him, 'Your will be done.' I believe God does not force us to do things but when we say in sincerity, 'Your will be done,' and open ourselves to him he can work through us in wonderful ways. Intercession is sharing our hopes and our fears, our joys and our sorrows with the Beloved in the knowledge that he cares for us all, and at the same time offering our lives to him that he might work through us. Our time of intercession can be a time when God speaks to us and sends us out to live and work to his praise and glory: through intercession we learn to work with God for the good of all.

Intercession is always in danger of becoming dull if it is just the same list time after time. Prayer is not dull. God can never be dull! So we need to make sure our asking prayers are full of life and love. Most of the intercessions in this book follow a simple structure, we pray in turn for the Church, the world, our families and friends, the ill and the suffering, and the departed. This is meant to be an aid to prayer and not a restrictive pattern. An all inclusive pattern for prayer cannot be exclusive when we are praying to God who loves all. The prayers are offered as an aid to your own prayers and not to replace your own prayers. They are not just to be read out; they are to be made your own and to be prayed from your heart. It is always good to find matters that concern you and events that are in the news to add to these prayers. Make sure that your intercessions are part of your living relationship with God. Above all let your intercessions be an affirmation of the presence and power of God and his love for all.

David Adam

Year A

First Sunday of Advent

YEAR A

Blessed are you, Lord our God,
for you have created us out of your love
and for your love.
You have given us eyes to see,
minds to understand
and hearts to love you.
Help us to be aware of your presence
and your coming to us
this day and always.

We ask your blessing
upon all preachers and ministers of the word,
that they may proclaim your presence
and the coming of your kingdom.
We remember before you
all who seek to witness to your abiding love
and your dwelling among us.
We pray for your faithful people
as they prepare to celebrate Christmas
and to rejoice in your love for them.

Silence

Come, Lord God,
make yourself known among us.

We pray for all who watch during the darkness of night
and seek our safety.
We remember the police, coastguards, fire crews,
the ambulance service and all doctors and nurses.
We ask your blessing
upon all who work through the night
to provide us with our daily needs.

Silence

Come, Lord God,
make yourself known among us.

We give you thanks for our homes and our loved ones.
At this time of preparation for Christmas
help us to make sure we have time
for each other and for you.
We remember all who will be lonely and troubled
at this time.

Silence

Come, Lord God,
make yourself known among us.

We give thanks for our health and well-being.
We remember in your presence
all who have suddenly become ill
or been injured in accidents,
and those whose lives have been darkened
by the loss of a loved one.
We ask your blessing
upon all who are homeless or hungry
and all who fear the future.
May they know your presence
and so have courage and hope in their troubles.

Silence

Come, Lord God,
make yourself known among us.

We rejoice that you come to us
and offer us life that is eternal.
We remember in your presence
our loved ones departed and all your saints.
May we all rejoice for ever in your love.

Silence

Merciful Father,
accept these prayers
for the sake of your Son,
our Saviour Jesus Christ.
Amen.

Second Sunday of Advent

YEAR A

Blessed are you, Lord our God,
for you sent the prophets and John the Baptist
to prepare your way.
You have told us of your coming
and you reveal yourself to us in Jesus.
You come to each of us in power and in love.
Blessed are you, Father, Son and Holy Spirit.

Father, we give thanks
for all who tell of your love
and who proclaim your coming.
We ask your blessing upon all priests and preachers,
upon all who teach the Scriptures
and tell of your coming.
Bless all who are baptised
into your presence and power.
Lord, we ask forgiveness
when your Church misuses
the resources you have given it
and when we fail to live up to your teaching and love.

Silence

Lord, come to us:
forgive us and guide us.

We remember in your presence
the troubles and sorrows of our world.
We pray for all who are caught up in war or violence,
all who suffer from the greed and insensitivity of others.
May we not misuse or squander the earth's resources
but use them with care and for the benefit of all.
We ask your blessing upon all leaders and politicians.

Silence

Lord, come to us:
forgive us and guide us.

We ask your blessing
upon all who do not look forward to Christmas.
We remember all who will be homeless or lonely
and all who are poor or deeply in debt.
We pray that our homes
may be places of love and peace
where you are welcome.
May we know that in the coming of others to us
you also come and seek our love.

Silence

Lord, come to us:
forgive us and guide us.

We remember all who are ill
and suffering at this time,
all who are distressed
and those who are overburdened.
May they know your peace and your presence.
May all who walk in darkness
come to know your light and your love.
We pray for all who are in hospital
or in care at this time.

Silence

Lord, come to us:
forgive us and guide us.

We remember all our loved ones departed,
and we pray for any who have died recently.
May they rejoice in the fullness of life
and be with you in glory.

Silence

Merciful Father,
accept these prayers
for the sake of your Son,
our Saviour Jesus Christ.
Amen.

Third Sunday of Advent

YEAR A

Blessed are you, Lord our God,
who has promised us your salvation
through the prophets,
and that in you we will find healing and peace.
We come to you,
for in our coming we turn away from the darkness
and enter into the light of your presence and your love.

Mighty God and Saviour,
we pray for your Church throughout the world,
that it may witness to you
not only in word but also in deed.
May the Church reflect your love for the world
and show your acceptance and forgiveness
for all peoples.
We remember at this time
all who are persecuted for their faith
and all who are prisoners of conscience.

Silence

Come, Lord,
for our hope is in you.

We remember in your presence
all who are oppressed by tyranny or evil.
We pray for those
who have been driven out of their homes
and who have been separated from loved ones.
We ask your blessing
on all who suffer from poverty or hunger
and all who are caught up in war
or live in fear of terrorism.

Silence

Come, Lord,
for our hope is in you.

We give thanks for those who have taught us the faith
by the example of the way they live.
May we be a good example to others.
Lord, bless our homes and our loved ones
with the light of your presence.
We remember all who are struggling in their relationships
and those whose minds are full of doubt.

Silence

Come, Lord,
for our hope is in you.

Lord, we come to you for renewal and healing,
for strength and for light.
We ask your blessing
upon all who suffer from a disability
or who are ill at this time.
We remember those who are blind, lame or deaf
and those who suffer from leprosy.
We pray for all who have lost loved ones this week
and for those who are caring for the terminally ill.

Silence

Come, Lord,
for our hope is in you.

We give thanks for your renewing powers
and that you give us life and life eternal.
We remember friends and loved ones
who are departed from us.
May they rejoice in fullness of life
and in the glory of your presence.

Silence

Merciful Father,
accept these prayers
for the sake of your Son,
our Saviour Jesus Christ.
Amen.

Fourth Sunday of Advent

YEAR A

Blessed are you, Lord our God,
for in your love you wait on us.
You trust us with your plans
and allow us to share in the bringing in of your kingdom.
Help us at all times to trust in you
and to seek to do your will.
Blessed are you, Father, Son and Holy Spirit.

Lord, ever with us, help your Church
to proclaim your presence and your saving power.
May we seek to do your will
and help to bring in your kingdom.
As we give thanks for Joseph,
we give thanks for all men and women of vision
and all who have dedicated their lives in your service.
We ask your blessing upon all preachers
and ministers of the sacraments.
Guide all who serve you quietly in their daily lives.
We remember especially
all who struggle to serve you
while surrounded by difficult circumstances
and opposition.

Silence

God, come among us:
make your home with us.

God of freedom,
we pray for all who are oppressed.
We ask your blessing upon all who suffer
through tyranny or terrorism.
We remember all whose freedom has been diminished
through war or violence.
We pray for the poor, the hungry and the homeless.

Silence

God, come among us:
make your home with us.

We give thanks for our homes
and for all who love us.
May we show your presence in our daily living.
We pray for homes where there is neglect or lack of love,
where there is cruelty or deep selfishness.
We remember all who live alone
and those who are lonely.

Silence

God, come among us:
make your home with us.

Lord, you are with us even when it is dark.
We ask your blessing
upon all who are in pain or in fear.
We pray for those who are ill at home or in hospital
and all who have been injured this week.
We remember those who feel life has little meaning
and those who have lost their way
or who are anxious about their future.

Silence

God, come among us:
make your home with us.

We give thanks that in you life is eternal
and we ask your blessing
upon our friends and loved ones
who are departed from us.

Silence

Merciful Father,
accept these prayers
for the sake of your Son,
our Saviour Jesus Christ.
Amen.

Christmas Day

YEAR A

Blessed are you, Lord our God,
for in Jesus Christ, the Word made flesh,
you share in our humanity.
You come among us to be one with us
and that we may come to you.
Blessed are you, Father, Son and Holy Spirit.

Lord God, we welcome you
into our hearts, our homes our lives.
We ask your blessing upon the Church
as it worships you throughout the world.
May it ever witness to your presence and your love.
Guide all preachers of the word
and ministers of the sacraments,
that they may lead us to you
and help us to know you and to love you.

Silence

Lord, come to us.
Save us and help us, O Lord.

We rejoice with the shepherds
and pray for peace on earth and goodwill
among all peoples.
We ask your blessing upon all areas
where there is war, conflict and oppression.
We remember those who are not at peace
with themselves or with others.
We pray for all who are disturbed or distressed.

Silence

Lord, come to us.
Save us and help us, O Lord.

Lord, born into an ordinary home, come to our homes,
that they may reflect your peace and your glory.
We ask your blessing upon all our loved ones,
those with whom we share this Christmas
and those who are not able to be with us.

Silence

Lord, come to us.
Save us and help us, O Lord.

We remember all who find this a stressful time.
We pray for the world poor
and those who are deeply in debt.
We remember before you the homeless
and we pray for the work of Shelter
and other relief organisations.
We seek your blessing upon all who are lonely
and those who feel neglected or forgotten at this time.
We remember also all who are ill and in hospital.

Silence

Lord, come to us.
Save us and help us, O Lord.

Lord, we rejoice that you came down to earth as a human,
that we might share in the joys of the kingdom of heaven.
We remember before you friends and loved ones departed,
especially those who have died this year.
We rejoice in the fellowship of Mary and Joseph
and all your saints.
May we share with them in your glory.

Silence

Merciful Father,
accept these prayers
for the sake of your Son,
our Saviour Jesus Christ.
Amen.

First Sunday of Christmas

YEAR A

Blessed are you, Lord our God,
for you are always ready to help and protect us.
You are a present help in all our needs and troubles.
Blessed are you, Father, Son and Holy Spirit.

God our Redeemer, we thank you
for the Church throughout the whole world.
We remember especially today
the Coptic Church of Egypt.
We ask your blessing upon all Christians
who are being persecuted or penalised for their faith.
We pray for Christians who are exiled
or imprisoned for their beliefs.
We remember all who are struggling with doubt
and those who lack any teaching in the faith.

Silence

God our Redeemer,
hear us and help us.

We give thanks for our land and its freedom.
We remember in your presence
all who are refugees or homeless at this time.
We ask your blessing upon the world poor
and all who are unable to use their abilities and talents.
Bless the work of Fair Trade organisations
and all who strive to relieve injustice and poverty.

Silence

God our Redeemer,
hear us and help us.

We give thanks for the love and protection of our parents.
We ask your blessing upon our homes
and all our loved ones,
that they may live in peace and be free from poverty.
We remember all children who have been taken into care
and all families who find it difficult to cope.
We pray for any parents who have lost a child
over this last year.

Silence

God our Redeemer,
hear us and help us.

We give thanks for the medical profession
and for all who care for our well-being.
We ask your blessing upon all who are ill
at home or in hospital.
We remember any who have been injured
in accidents or through acts of violence.
We pray especially for families
where there is a child who is ill or suffering.

Silence

God our Redeemer,
hear us and help us.

We give thanks that you are our Redeemer;
that you seek that we should not perish
but have everlasting life.
We remember friends and loved ones
who are departed from us.
We rejoice in the fellowship of all your saints
and ask that we may share with them in your glory.

Silence

Merciful Father,
accept these prayers
for the sake of your Son,
our Saviour Jesus Christ.
Amen.

Second Sunday of Christmas

YEAR A

Blessed are you, Lord God,
Creator of heaven and earth.
In you and in your love
heaven and earth are one.
You have sent your Son, our Saviour,
to lead us back into your kingdom.
You have called us to work with you
and have given us of your Spirit.
Blessed are you, Father, Son and Holy Spirit.

We give you thanks and praise
that we may share in your kingdom here on earth
and that in Jesus Christ
we see our humanity and your divinity as one.
We ask your blessing upon all preachers of the word,
on all who proclaim your presence
by their actions and their love.
We pray for all who are seekers
and that we may know you better and love you more.
We remember all who are being prepared
for baptism or confirmation
and all who are seeking
to commit their lives to you in love.

Silence

Holy God, come among us:
hear us and help us.

We pray for peace on earth and goodwill among all people.
We ask your blessing upon all who strive for justice and peace.
We pray for the United Nations
and all who seek to bring unity and fellowship
between nations.

Silence

Holy God, come among us:
hear us and help us.

We give thanks that Jesus was born into an earthly home
and shared in our daily life.
May we know that our homes and loved ones
are part of your kingdom.
We ask your blessing on homes
where there is strife and division, deceit and distrust.

Silence

Holy God, come among us:
hear us and help us.

We give thanks that nothing can separate us
from your love.
We ask your blessing upon all
who are ill, lonely or oppressed.
We remember friends and loved ones
who are in hospital or ill at home
and all who are caring for them.
We pray also for all who despair,
all who have lost hope or any vision of your love.

Silence

Holy God, come among us:
hear us and help us.

Loving God, you invite us to delight in your presence
and to live in your kingdom.
Lord, keep us in life eternal.
We give thanks for your faithful ones departed
and we rejoice in the fellowship of all your saints.

Silence

Merciful Father,
accept these prayers
for the sake of your Son,
our Saviour Jesus Christ.
Amen.

The Epiphany

YEAR A

Blessed are you, Lord our God,
for you have called us to seek you,
to know and to love you.
You have revealed yourself in Jesus Christ,
our Saviour and our God.
We come to worship you.
Blessed are you, Father, Son and Holy Spirit.

We give thanks for the wise men
and the leading of a star.
We ask your blessing upon all who are seekers
and all who dedicate their lives to you.
We remember all those who lead worship
and teach of your love and salvation.
We pray today especially for the Churches of the Far East.

Silence

Lord, we seek you and call upon you:
hear us and help us.

As the wise men sought a king, we rejoice
that you are the King of kings and Lord of lords.
May your love and your will rule in our hearts.
We ask your blessing upon all leaders of people
and all who make important decisions for our world.
We pray today for all research scientists.

Silence

Lord, we seek you and call upon you:
hear us and help us.

As the Holy Family shared in an ordinary home,
we ask your blessing upon our homes.
May our homes reveal your presence
and our relationships increase our love for you.
We remember all homeless peoples,
all refugees and those who belong to homes
where there is violence or lack of love.

Silence

Lord, we seek you and call upon you:
hear us and help us.

With the gift of myrrh
there was an offering of the sorrows of our world.
We remember all who long for freedom and redemption.
We pray for all suffering people,
all who are distressed
and all who feel that no one cares for them.
We pray for the work of doctors, nurses, paramedics
and all who are involved in healing.

Silence

Lord, we seek you and call upon you:
hear us and help us.

We rejoice with Mary and Joseph,
with the shepherds and the angels,
with the wise men,
with the Church in heaven and on earth.
We commend ourselves, all peoples and the whole world
to your unfailing love.

Silence

Merciful Father,
accept these prayers
for the sake of your Son,
our Saviour Jesus Christ.
Amen.

First Sunday of Epiphany

The Baptism of Christ

YEAR A

Blessed are you, Lord our God,
for you are our Maker, our Saviour and our Guide.
Keep us mindful of your presence,
your love and your power,
that we may learn to rejoice in you and your love.
Blessed are you, Father, Son and Holy Spirit.

We remember before you all who are being prepared
for baptism or confirmation.
We ask your blessing upon all who seek to reveal
your love and your peace.
We pray for all preachers of the word
and all who reach out in mission.
We pray that the Church may share in your mission to the world.
Lord, help us all to reveal your glory in our midst.

Silence

Holy Trinity,
hear us and help us.

We ask your blessing upon all who are beginning
new ventures and new work.
We pray for all who are being asked to extend themselves
through learning and the development of their abilities.
We remember those who are entering into new relationships
and we ask your blessing upon those who are newly married.

Silence

Holy Trinity,
hear us and help us.

We thank you for our homes and our loved ones.
We ask your blessing upon those who are moving to a new home
or who are moving away from their families.
We remember all who are homeless,
all who live in poverty or hunger.
We pray to you for all who work
to relieve the needs and suffering of others.

Silence

Holy Trinity,
hear us and help us.

We remember before you
all who feel confused or troubled at this time.
We pray for all who are distressed
and those who are not able to cope
with what is happening around them.
May they know your presence and your power.
We ask your blessing upon all who are ill
at home or in hospital,
especially those who are fearful or lonely.

Silence

Holy Trinity,
hear us and help us.

We rejoice in the gift of life and life eternal.
We ask your blessing upon our loved ones and friends
who have departed from us.
We remember especially today
those who have enriched our lives
by their example and goodness.
May they rejoice in glory
and may we share with them in your eternal kingdom.

Silence

Merciful Father,
accept these prayers
for the sake of your Son,
our Saviour Jesus Christ.
Amen.

Second Sunday of Epiphany

YEAR A

Blessed are you, Lord our God,
for you have called us to know you
and to abide with you.
You have called us to love you and to tell of you.
Blessed are you, Father, Son and Holy Spirit,
for you have called us into life and life eternal.
Blessed be God for ever.

Father, we ask your blessing upon the Church,
that it may grow in love for you,
that it may grow in holiness,
that it may grow in size.
We remember before you
all who reach out in mission
to tell of your love and your saving power.
We pray for preachers of the word
and teachers of the faith,
and we ask that we may all share
in bringing others to you.

Silence

Lord, we pray to you:
you are our health and salvation.

Lord God,
we pray for all who are being exploited by others.
We remember the poor and the homeless
and we ask your blessing
upon all who care for refugees and deprived peoples.
We pray for all who lack any moral or spiritual guidance
and who are being led astray by people around them.

Silence

Lord, we pray to you:
you are our health and salvation.

We give thanks for those who taught us the faith
and who set us an example by their lives.
We ask your blessing upon our home,
our loved ones and all who have cared for us.
We pray for all who suffer from neglect, violence
or a lack of love.

Silence

Lord, we pray to you:
you are our health and salvation.

God, in you is our peace and our hope.
We remember in your presence
all who are ill or suffering.
We pray especially for any who feel confused by life
and who are not able to cope.
We pray for all who are caught up in drug abuse or vice.

Silence

Lord, we pray to you:
you are our health and salvation.

We give thanks for your redeeming love
and for the gift of life eternal.
We pray for all our loved ones departed
and commend them, this world and ourselves
to your unfailing love.

Silence

Merciful Father,
accept these prayers
for the sake of your Son,
our Saviour Jesus Christ.
Amen.

Third Sunday of Epiphany

YEAR A

Blessed are you, Lord our God,
for you give us life,
you give us love,
you give us yourself.
Lord, may we learn to give our life, our love,
ourselves to you, for it is in such giving
that we open our lives to you.
Blessed are you, Father, Son and Holy Spirit.

We give you thanks, O Lord,
for all who have heard your call
and served you faithfully.
We give thanks
for those who have shared their faith with us.
We ask your blessing upon all who seek to witness
to your abiding presence and your love.
We pray for all who are seeking to fulfil their calling in life.
We pray for schools, colleges and universities.
We remember especially today
all who are being prepared for baptism,
confirmation or ordination.

Silence

Lord, hear us
and help us to serve you.

We give thanks for all who provide us with our daily food.
We ask your blessing upon all who are involved
in growing or supplying our food.
We remember before you
all who are being used as cheap labour
and we pray for fair trade and justice.
May we all use the resources of the world
with care and respect.

Silence

Lord, hear us
and help us to serve you.

We give thanks for our homes and our loved ones,
for all who have enriched us
by their love and generosity.
We ask your blessing upon all who are struggling
through debt, poverty or homelessness.
We pray for all who feel used, abused or unloved.

Silence

Lord, hear us
and help us to serve you.

We ask your blessing
upon all who are finding life difficult
through illness or oppression.
We pray for all who feel their abilities
are being wasted or thwarted
through illness or circumstance.
May we know that in whatever circumstance
we find ourselves
God still loves us and calls us to love him.

Silence

Lord, hear us
and help us to serve you.

We rejoice that we are called to life eternal.
We remember friends and loved ones
who are departed from us.
May we all share in your abiding love
and the fullness of life eternal.

Silence

Merciful Father,
accept these prayers
for the sake of your Son,
our Saviour Jesus Christ.
Amen.

Fourth Sunday of Epiphany

(Also for use on the Feast of the Presentation)

YEAR A

Blessed are you, Lord our God.
You give us life
and you continually renew and refresh us
with your presence and your love.
You are the strength of the weak
and the light to all who walk in darkness.
Blessed are you, Father, Son and Holy Spirit.

Lord God, may we reveal your joy and power
in our daily living.
We ask your blessing upon the Church,
that it may be obedient to your word
and seek to bring others to know your glory.
We ask you to bless all preachers and teachers of the faith,
that they may have the power
to reveal you and your love to others.

Silence

God of love and joy,
hear us and refresh us.

Lord, our Creator,
we pray that we may use the world aright.
Let us not squander or waste the resources you have given us
but use them to your glory and the benefit of all.
We pray for all who monitor our planet and its resources.
We ask your blessing upon scientists and politicians
and all who work to care for and improve our world.
We remember today
all who suffer from deprivation, from poverty,
from hunger or from homelessness.

Silence

God of love and joy,
hear us and refresh us.

We give thanks for our own home
and all you have given us.
We pray for those who provide us with our food
and our daily needs.
We ask your blessing upon all who work
to provide good homes and shelter
to the poor of our world.

Silence

God of love and joy,
hear us and refresh us.

We remember today all who are running out of resources.
We pray for the fearful and the anxious,
the sad and the lonely.
We ask your blessing upon all who are ill
and cannot cope on their own.
We remember all who, through ageing or illness,
need regular care and attention.
We pray for all carers
and all who work in the health service.

Silence

God of love and joy,
hear us and refresh us.

We rejoice in life and that you give us life eternal.
Renewing and restoring God,
we remember in your presence our loved ones departed
and ask that they may rejoice in your presence
and in the fullness of life eternal.
We commend them, the world and ourselves
to your unfailing love.

Silence

Merciful Father,
accept these prayers
for the sake of your Son,
our Saviour Jesus Christ.
Amen.

The Presentation of Christ

(To be used on the Sunday nearest 2 February, if not on the day)

YEAR A

Blessed are you, Lord God.
To you be all praise and glory for ever and ever,
for you are our light and our salvation.
You created light out of darkness
and have brought your light to our lives
through the birth of your Son, our Lord Jesus Christ.
Blessed are you, Father, Son and Holy Spirit,
one God for ever and ever.

As our Lord was brought into the Temple,
we ask your blessing upon the Church
throughout the world.
May we share in the mission of Christ
and show that his light is for all peoples and nations.
We remember all who are being baptised or confirmed
and all who are seeking to dedicate their lives
in your service.
We pray for all your faithful people,
that they may be lights in the world.

Silence

Lord of light and life,
hear our prayer.

Lord, we pray for the time
when the kingdoms of this world
may become the kingdom of Christ our Lord.
We ask your blessing upon Elizabeth our queen
and upon all leaders and rulers of nations.
Lord, give wisdom to all who are in authority.
We pray for all who influence our minds
through the press and the media.

Silence

Lord of light and life,
hear our prayer.

As Joseph and Mary presented Jesus in the Temple,
we ask your blessing upon our young people,
that they may be taught the faith and learn to love you.
We remember before you our own homes and loved ones.
We pray for all schools, colleges and universities.

Silence

Lord of light and life,
hear our prayer.

We remember all who walk in darkness.
We pray for those who are fearful, anxious or depressed.
We ask your blessing upon the world poor,
the persecuted, the hungry, the refugees, the homeless,
and all whose lives are in danger.
We pray for all who are ill at home or in hospital.

Silence

Lord of light and life,
hear our prayer.

We rejoice in the fellowship of all your saints
and ask your blessing upon our loved ones and friends
who are departed from us.
May they rejoice in your light
and in the fullness of life eternal.

Silence

Merciful Father,
accept these prayers
for the sake of your Son,
our Saviour Jesus Christ.
Amen.

Proper 1

Sunday between 3 and 9 February inclusive
(if earlier than the Second Sunday before Lent)

YEAR A

Blessed are you, Lord God,
Giver of life and Creator of love.
We give you thanks and praise for the light of each day
and for the light of the Gospel
as revealed in our Saviour Jesus Christ.
We rejoice in the life that you give us
and we delight in your presence.
Blessed are you, Father, Son and Holy Spirit.

As we give thanks for the light of Jesus Christ
we ask that this light may shine in our lives
and in the whole Church.
We ask your blessing on all who proclaim the Gospel
and who teach the word.
We pray for all who are seeking
to revive and promote faith in you and your love.
May the Church grow in love, in witness and in number.

Silence

Lord God of light,
scatter the darkness from our world.

We ask your blessing upon rulers and leaders
who have difficult decisions to make concerning the world
and who are often not sure which way to go.
We pray for all who work
to bring freedom and justice to all people,
those who seek to relieve the poor
and care for the oppressed.
We pray for those who feel
that they are working in the dark
and unable to find their way.

Silence

Lord God of light,
scatter the darkness from our world.

Lord, we ask that all darkness be dispersed
from our hearts and our communities.
May we help to bring your light and life
to our homes and to all our relationships.
We ask your blessing upon our families and friends
and upon all with whom we work or play.

Silence

Lord God of light,
scatter the darkness from our world.

We remember today all who walk in darkness
and in the shadow of fear or death.
We ask your blessing upon the fearful,
the anxious and the troubled.
We pray for all who are in the darkness
of doubt or despair.
We bring before you friends and loved ones who are ill
or who are finding it hard to cope with life.

Silence

Lord God of light,
scatter the darkness from our world.

We give thanks for the fullness of eternal life.
We ask your blessing upon our loved ones
who have entered into the fullness of your kingdom
and all the faithful departed.
We pray for the day when we may all see you more clearly
and walk without fear in your light.

Silence

Merciful Father,
accept these prayers
for the sake of your Son,
our Saviour Jesus Christ.
Amen.

Proper 2

Sunday between 10 and 16 February inclusive
(if earlier than the Second Sunday before Lent)

YEAR A

Blessed are you, Lord our God,
for you have created us in your own image:
you have called us to reflect
your love and your forgiveness to all.
You give us power to share in your grace.
Blessed are you, Father, Son and Holy Spirit.

Lord, as you reveal your love to us,
help us to show that love
towards all whom we meet.
We ask your blessing
upon all who seek to reveal your grace
and to walk in the way of your laws.
We remember before you
all who preach and teach of your love.
We ask your blessing
upon all who study the Scriptures
in groups or in schools.

Silence

Lord of life and love,
hear us and help us.

Lord, as you teach us to respect each other,
help us to respect the earth and all its creatures.
Give us a reverence towards all of your creation.
Guide all who care for the resources of our planet
and the environment in which we live.
We pray for areas that have been devastated
by war or greed.

Silence

Lord of life and love,
hear us and help us.

Lord, forgive our times of anger and hatred
and help us to live at peace with each other.
May our communities be places
where no one is belittled and no one oppressed.
We pray for our homes and our loved ones.

Silence

Lord of life and love,
hear us and help us.

Lord, we remember before you
all who are suffering through violence or abuse.
We pray especially for those
whose lives are marred by their past or present sins.
We remember also today all who are struggling
with pain or chronic illness
and all who can no longer cope with life on their own.

Silence

Lord of life and love,
hear us and help us.

We rejoice that nothing can separate us
from the love of God in Christ Jesus.
We ask your blessing
upon our friends and loved ones departed.
As we rejoice in the fellowship of all your saints,
we commend this world, all peoples and ourselves
to your unfailing love.

Silence

Merciful Father,
accept these prayers
for the sake of your Son,
our Saviour Jesus Christ.
Amen.

Proper 3

Sunday between 17 and 23 February inclusive
(if earlier than the Second Sunday before Lent)

YEAR A

Blessed are you, Lord God, King of the Universe,
for you have created us in your own image.
You have called us to reflect your love
and your forgiveness to all.
Blessed are you, Father, Son and Holy Spirit.

We pray that your Church may reflect
your love and your mercy;
that we may live as those who share
your peace and your forgiveness;
that we may seek to live in harmony and peace
with each other;
that we will be known as Christians by our love.

Silence

Living and loving God,
hear us and help us.

We ask your blessing upon all who are suffering
from acts of violence and war at this time.
We remember all who are suffering
through the anger and hatred of others.
Lord, may they not be overcome with evil
but overcome evil with good.
We pray for the work of the United Nations
and all peacekeeping forces.

Silence

Living and loving God,
hear us and help us.

Lord, we thank you
for all who have shown us the way of love
through their own self-giving and generosity.
We ask your blessing upon our homes
and all who are dear to us.
We remember before you
all who are denied human love
or who feel rejected at this time.

Silence

Living and loving God,
hear us and help us.

We remember all whose lives are being destroyed
by hatred and resentment,
all who are caught up in violence and war.
We pray for all who are suffering in our world,
especially those who feel they are on their own
without help.
We ask your blessing upon all who work
for the relief of suffering and sorrow.

Silence

Living and loving God,
hear us and help us.

We rejoice in the fellowship of your saints
and all who have reflected your image here on earth.
We pray for friends and loved ones
who have enriched our lives
and are now departed from us.
Lord, we commit ourselves, all on earth and in heaven
to you and your unfailing love.

Silence

Merciful Father,
accept these prayers
for the sake of your Son,
our Saviour Jesus Christ.
Amen.

Second Sunday before Lent

YEAR A

Blessed are you, Lord God,
for you are our Creator and Redeemer;
you are our Strength and Shield.
As you love us with an everlasting love
and offer us life eternal,
help us to trust in you and in your grace.
Blessed are you, Father, Son and Holy Spirit.

Lord, help us to love the world
with the great love that you have for the world.
Guide your Church, that it may keep its priorities
and that above all it may seek you and your will
in all that it does.
Lord, increase our faith in you,
that we may reveal your presence in our lives.
We ask your blessing
upon all who are suffering for their beliefs
or who are struggling with their faith.

Silence

Lord God, hear us:
help us to put our trust in you.

Father, we thank you for the beauty of the earth,
for flowers and birds.
We pray for all who seek to conserve and protect
the world in which we live.
We ask your blessing upon all who deal with limited resources,
upon those who care for fish stocks,
and those who deal with the rainforests.
We pray for all who are short of food
or deprived of proper homes.

Silence

Lord God, hear us:
help us to put our trust in you.

We give thanks for our lives
and your love towards us.
Lord, bless our families and friends with your goodness.
May the way we live show our trust in you.
Let us not squander or hoard
the good things you have given us
but use them to the good and benefit of all.

Silence

Lord God, hear us:
help us to put our trust in you.

God of love and peace, we remember before you
all who are weighed down with anxiety or fear.
We pray for those who are depressed
and those who feel they can no longer cope with life.
We ask your blessing upon all who are ill
and all who suffer in any way.
May they come to know your love and your peace.

Silence

Lord God, hear us:
help us to put our trust in you.

We give thanks for your everlasting love
and we rejoice in the gift of eternal life.
Lord, we commend to you
our friends and loved ones who are departed from us.
May they enjoy your presence and your love.
We commit them, this world and ourselves
to your unfailing presence and peace.

Silence

Merciful Father,
accept these prayers
for the sake of your Son,
our Saviour Jesus Christ.
Amen.

Sunday before Lent

YEAR A

Blessed are you, Lord God,
ever present in our lives.
Through the power of your Spirit
you reveal your glory to us
in the face of Jesus Christ.
Help us to trust in you
and in the power of the resurrection.
Blessed are you, Father, Son and Holy Spirit.

Lord, guide your Church,
that in its words and actions
it may reveal your glory.
We ask your blessing
upon preachers of the word
and ministers of the sacraments,
that they may help us to do your will
and to have a vision of your purpose,
and that each in our mission
may proclaim your kingdom and your glory.

Silence

God, in your goodness,
grant us a glimpse of your glory.

We remember all who have lost their way
and who feel confused by life,
especially those who feel life has no meaning or purpose.
We pray for all who are captives of vice or drugs.
We ask your blessing
upon all who are fearful,
especially those who are suffering
from persecution or poverty.

Silence

God, in your goodness,
grant us a glimpse of your glory.

Lord, change us and we shall be changed.
Transform our homes into places of your glory.
Transform our lives to reveal your presence.
Transform our minds to know your peace.
Transform our hearts to abide in your love.
May we know you are always with our loved ones
and with us.

Silence

God, in your goodness,
grant us a glimpse of your glory.

Lord, transform our darkness with your light.
We ask your blessing
upon all who are struggling with illness
or who are no longer able to cope on their own.
We pray for all who have been injured
in accidents or through violence this week.
We pray for the work of the rescue services
and all who seek to bring and maintain peace.

Silence

God, in your goodness,
grant us a glimpse of your glory.

We rejoice in your power
and in the resurrection.
We pray for friends and loved ones departed,
that they may enjoy and rest in your glory.
We seek to share in the fellowship
of all your saints in glory.

Silence

Merciful Father,
accept these prayers
for the sake of your Son,
our Saviour Jesus Christ.
Amen.

First Sunday of Lent

YEAR A

Blessed are you, Lord our God,
for you give us grace to defeat evil
and to resist temptation.
In our troubles you are our strength and our support.
You bring us to eternal life.
Blessed are you, Father, Son and Holy Spirit,
for ever and ever.

Lord, bless your people who are struggling with temptation.
Guide your Church, that it may lead others to do your will
and to live in love and peace with all.
Lord, help us to make others aware
of the deep spiritual things within our world:
that we are all called to work with you.
Help us to do your will
and so live in your kingdom.

Silence

Lord, hear us
and deliver us from evil.

We remember before you
all who are suffering through sin, violence and war.
We pray for peoples and nations
that are divided against each other
through ancient wrongs and through greed.
We pray for all who are sorely tempted to do wrong.
Lord, show us all the peace we should give
and the peace we should forgo.

Silence

Lord, hear us
and deliver us from evil.

We ask your blessing upon our homes and families.
We bring before you all who are suffering
from broken relationships and broken homes.
We pray for those who have been rejected
by their families
and all who feel they have been betrayed in love.
Bless all who work to bring reconciliation
and new hope to separated peoples.

Silence

Lord, hear us
and deliver us from evil.

We give thanks for all who share in healing
and the restoring of well-being to all who suffer.
We remember all who are in pain
or distress at this time.
We ask your blessing
upon all who are separated from loved ones
through illness or disability
and all who can no longer cope on their own.

Silence

Lord, hear us
and deliver us from evil.

We give thanks for the forgiveness of sins
and the hope of eternal life.
We rejoice in the fellowship
of all the saints and the faithful
who are now in your kingdom.
We pray for our loved ones departed.
May we all at the last share in the glory
of your kingdom and your love.

Silence

Merciful Father,
accept these prayers
for the sake of your Son,
our Saviour Jesus Christ.
Amen.

Second Sunday of Lent

YEAR A

Blessed are you, Lord our God,
for you have called us out of darkness
to be children of light.
The bright light of your presence
scatters the darkness within us
and is a guide on our journey.
Blessed are you, Father, Son and Holy Spirit.

We rejoice that in Christ we know
that light is stronger than darkness
and life is stronger than death.
Give your Church the courage
to proclaim the Good News to all people.
We remember all who are in doubt
or who are struggling with their faith.
We pray for those who have lost faith
and walk in darkness.

Silence

Lord, hear us:
come, lighten our darkness.

Lord of all, we bring before you
the troubles and dangers of peoples and nations,
the war-torn and the world-weary.
We ask your blessing
upon communities seeking to rebuild their lives
in peace and hope.
We pray for all rulers, governments
and leaders of people,
that they will strive for justice and peace.

Silence

Lord, hear us:
come, lighten our darkness.

Bless our homes with the light of your presence.
We pray for our loved ones and friends,
for our neighbours and our community.
May the bright light of Christ shine within us
and scatter any darkness that is around us.

Silence

Lord, hear us:
come, lighten our darkness.

We remember all who are struggling
with illness or with fear.
We ask your blessing
upon all who are in hospital,
all who have been injured
through violence or accidents.
We pray for all who are fearful of the future.
We pray also for the bereaved and the lonely.

Silence

Lord, hear us:
come, lighten our darkness.

We remember all who are nearing death
and those who care for them.
May they trust in you and in eternal life.
We commend all our loved ones departed
to your love and your kingdom.

Silence

Merciful Father,
accept these prayers
for the sake of your Son,
our Saviour Jesus Christ.
Amen.

Third Sunday of Lent

YEAR A

Blessed are you, Lord our God,
for you have made us for yourself and for your love.
We seek your presence
and desire to give our lives and our love to you.
Blessed are you, Father, Son and Holy Spirit.

Lord, may your presence be revealed
through your Church.
May we never be satisfied with words without content,
with actions without love,
with buildings that do not convey your presence.
Lord, fill us and make us a holy people,
a fulfilled people and a missionary people.
Bless the Church,
that it may grow in outreach, in holiness and in number.

Silence

Lord, we look for you; we long for you:
come fill us with your Spirit.

You have given us a wonderful world.
Let us not spoil it through greed or lack of respect.
We remember all who suffer from hunger and thirst.
We pray for all who do not have proper water supplies
or who have to walk miles to get water.
We pray also for all in the consumer society
who try to fill their lives with things
and are never satisfied.

Silence

Lord, we look for you; we long for you:
come fill us with your Spirit.

We give thanks for the longings that you have given us.
We ask your blessing upon our loved ones,
our families and friends.
We remember before you all who are lonely,
those who are failing in health or strength,
and all who are fearful for the future.

Silence

Lord, we look for you; we long for you:
come fill us with your Spirit.

We give thanks for the joy and freedom
you give to our lives.
We pray for all who have become captives
to vice and drugs,
all who are suffering from the misuse of alcohol.
We remember their families who also suffer.
We ask your blessing upon all who are ill
and upon those who care for them.

Silence

Lord, we look for you; we long for you:
come fill us with your Spirit.

In the power of your Spirit
you renew and refresh us.
We pray for all who are departed from us,
that they may rejoice in the fullness of life eternal.
To you, O God, and your love
we commit this world, our loved ones and ourselves
now and for eternity.

Silence

Merciful Father,
accept these prayers
for the sake of your Son,
our Saviour Jesus Christ.
Amen.

Fourth Sunday of Lent
Mothering Sunday
YEAR A

Blessed are you, Lord our God,
for you have created us all.
We are your children,
loved by you
and ever under your care and protection.
We thank you for our life, your love
and all that you give us.
Blessed are you, Father, Son and Holy Spirit.

We thank you for the Church
that tells of your love
and helps people to know you.
Loving God, bless our Church,
that it may show your love to all who come to it.
We remember especially today
any who would have liked to be here
but were not able to come.

Silence

Life-giving and loving God,
hear us and help us.

We thank you for the wonderful world
that you have given us,
for the air we breathe and for water.
We thank you for all growing things and for food.
God bless all who work hard
to provide us with what we need.
We pray especially for hungry and homeless people.

Silence

Life-giving and loving God,
hear us and help us.

We thank you God for the love of our homes.
Thank you for the love and care of our mother.
We pray for families where a loved one is ill
or causing trouble.
We remember all who are suffering from lack of love,
and those who live in homes where there is tension
and broken relationships.

Silence

Life-giving and loving God,
hear us and help us.

We thank you for the confidence and joy we have
through knowing we are loved.
We ask your blessing
upon all who are lonely or neglected.
We pray for those separated from their loved ones
through illness or circumstance.
We pray for all who have been taken into care.

Silence

Life-giving and loving God,
hear us and help us.

We give thanks for your eternal love
and we pray to you for all our loved ones departed.
We remember all who have enriched our lives
by their goodness.
We commit our loved ones and all people
to your unfailing love.

Silence

Merciful Father,
accept these prayers
for the sake of your Son,
our Saviour Jesus Christ.
Amen.

Fifth Sunday of Lent

YEAR A

Blessed are you, Lord our God,
who sent your Son to be our Saviour.
In your love you have opened for us
the way to eternal life
and rescued us from perishing.
Blessed are you, Father, Son and Holy Spirit.

Come, Lord, to refresh and renew your Church,
which without you is dull and dry.
Come fill the Church,
which without you is dead.
Fill the Church with your life-giving presence
and give it the power
to proclaim the resurrection to eternal life.
Lord, renew our faith in you.
Give to your Church a new sense of mission and outreach.
Bless all preachers and ministers of the sacraments
with the joy of the Good News.

Silence

Come, Lord, revive us,
renew your people.

Come, Lord, be known
in all who share in your saving purpose.
Guide and bless all rescue workers.
We remember doctors and nurses,
ambulance workers and paramedics.
We pray for the fire service, the people on lifeboats
and all who risk their lives
in the care and service of others.
We pray for all who are carers within our communities.

Silence

Come, Lord, revive us,
renew your people.

Come, Lord, let your presence be known
in our homes and in our lives.
Bless us in all our relationships
and dealings with others.
Come, Lord, with your light and love
to lives that are struggling with poverty and debt,
with bad housing and broken-down communities.

Silence

Come, Lord, revive us,
renew your people.

Come, Lord, to all whose hope is gone,
the lost, the despairing and the deeply depressed.
We remember the over-worked, the world-weary,
the exhausted and the worn-out.
We ask your blessing
upon those who feel wrung out and dry,
all who feel numb
and those whose senses are deadened.
We pray for all suffering from deep stress or trauma
and their loved ones caring for them.

Silence

Come, Lord, revive us,
renew your people.

We give thanks for the hope of life eternal.
We remember in your presence
our friends and loved ones departed.
May we all come to know the joys of your kingdom
and the fullness of life eternal.

Silence

Merciful Father,
accept these prayers
for the sake of your Son,
our Saviour Jesus Christ.
Amen.

Palm Sunday

YEAR A

Blessed are you, Lord God of our salvation;
to you be praise and glory for ever.
As we rejoice this day
in the triumphant entry into Jerusalem,
may we too be willing to walk the way of the cross.
By our lives may we witness to you as our Lord and King
and declare your saving love to the world.
Blessed are you, Father, Son and Holy Spirit.

Come, Lord.
Cleanse your Church from any pride or greed.
Cleanse us from our sins and free us to serve you.
Strengthen our sense of mission and service.
Strengthen our sensitivity towards the needs of others.
Strengthen our faith and our vision for your world.

Silence

Saviour of the world, our Redeemer,
save us and help us.

Come, Lord.
Guide the nations into the ways of justice and peace.
Guide all leaders and rulers to care for our world.
Comfort all who are broken by war and violence.
Comfort all who are shattered
by the betrayal of loved ones;
all who feel scorned and rejected.
Comfort all who are imprisoned and wrongly sentenced.

Silence

Saviour of the world, our Redeemer,
save us and help us.

Come, Lord.
As our Saviour and Friend,
bless our homes and our loved ones with your love.
Guide us in all our dealings
and help us to live with you as our Lord.
Let your kingly rule be known in us
as it is in heaven.

Silence

Saviour of the world, our Redeemer,
save us and help us.

Come, Lord.
You were broken on the cross to make us whole.
Be with all who are suffering at this time.
Come as light to those who walk in darkness,
the despairing and the despondent.
Come as joy to all who have lost confidence
and to all who are depressed.
Come as hope to all who are ill
and fearful of their future.

Silence

Saviour of the world, our Redeemer,
save us and help us.

Lord Jesus, we remember that you died
that we might live.
You descended into the depths
to raise us to the heights.
We ask your blessing
upon all our loved ones departed.
May they rejoice in the fullness of your kingdom.

Silence

Merciful Father,
accept these prayers
for the sake of your Son,
our Saviour Jesus Christ.
Amen.

Easter Day

YEAR A

Blessed are you, Lord God,
by whose power our Lord Jesus is raised from the dead.
In your presence is life and life eternal.
In your power death is conquered
and the gate to eternal life is opened.
In your presence is the fullness of joy.
Blessed are you, Father, Son and Holy Spirit.

Lord, make us aware of your risen presence in our lives.
May our worship be full of joy and awe.
Give us the courage to go out
to proclaim your love and your saving power.
Lord, as we celebrate your resurrection,
strengthen your Church
to tell the Good News to the whole world.
Bless all who are called to teach and preach in your name.
In the power of the risen Lord,
may they lead us from darkness to his glorious light.

Silence

Risen Lord,
deliver us from the dominion
of darkness and death.

Lord Jesus, as we rejoice in your risen presence,
we pray that the world may know your peace.
May we rise above division and strife,
that your victory over darkness and death
may be known in the world.
Lord, show us the peace we should give,
the peace we should share
and the peace we must forgo.

Silence

Risen Lord,
deliver us from the dominion
of darkness and death.

Risen Lord, you appeared to the two Marys
and sent them to tell the disciples.
Help us to show your presence in our homes
and in all our dealings.
Let us walk and work in your presence
and seek to reveal your glory in the world.
We ask you to bless all our loved ones and friends
and keep us ever in your love.

Silence

Risen Lord,
deliver us from the dominion
of darkness and death.

We remember all who walk in darkness
and who are heavily burdened.
We pray for all who have lost hope and who despair.
We ask your blessing upon all who are chronically ill
and those who can no longer cope on their own.
We pray for all who are approaching death
and their loved ones who are caring for them.

Silence

Risen Lord,
deliver us from the dominion
of darkness and death.

Risen Lord, we ask that we might share in your resurrection
and triumph over darkness and death.
We ask your blessing upon our friends and loved ones
who are departed from us.
May they have a share with your saints in glory.
This day we rejoice that death is conquered:
we are free, for Christ has won the victory.

Silence

Merciful Father,
accept these prayers
for the sake of your Son,
our Saviour Jesus Christ.
Amen.

Second Sunday of Easter

YEAR A

Blessed are you,
God and Father of our Lord Jesus Christ.
To you be glory and praise for ever.
By raising your Son from the dead,
death has been destroyed
and new life has been restored.
In him the victory over sin and the grave is won.
As you call us to newness of life,
may our lives reflect his glory.
Blessed are you, Father, Son and Holy Spirit.

Lord, bless your Church,
that it may reveal your presence
and the power of the resurrection.
May each church community
show signs of new life and joy in you.
Through our relationship with you
may we bring others to be faithful.
We ask your blessing upon all who are seekers,
all who are new in the faith and all who are struggling
with doubt and darkness.

Silence

Lord, be known among us;
make haste to help us.

Lord, bless the world with your peace,
the peace that it cannot achieve on its own.
We pray for peace between nations and peoples.
We ask your blessing upon all peacemakers
and the work of the United Nations.
We pray for all who live in fear for their lives
and all who have lost confidence in themselves
or the world around them.

Silence

Lord, be known among us;
make haste to help us.

Lord, bless our homes and families
with the joy of your presence.
May our homes be ever open to you and your love.
We remember today all who suffer
from poverty or homelessness.
We ask your blessing upon all
who live amid strife and fear
and all who are unable to rejoice in life.

Silence

Lord, be known among us;
make haste to help us.

Lord, bless all who feel restricted
by what is happening around them.
We remember all who live in violent or deprived areas.
We ask your blessing upon all who are ill
or who have been injured through accidents,
and upon those who care for them.
Lord, give them courage and hope in their troubles.

Silence

Lord, be known among us;
make haste to help us.

Lord of life and life eternal,
bless our loved ones departed,
that in fellowship with all your saints
they may rejoice in the fullness
of your presence and glory.

Silence

Merciful Father,
accept these prayers
for the sake of your Son,
our Saviour Jesus Christ.
Amen.

Third Sunday of Easter

YEAR A

Blessed are you, Lord God,
for you are with us in our journeying and in our resting.
You are to be found in our homes and our daily lives.
You, Lord, are our hope and our strength:
in you we trust.
Blessed are you, Father, Son and Holy Spirit.

Lord, make yourself known to us
in church and through the Scriptures.
May we know you in the breaking of the bread,
in the break of day
and when our hearts are breaking.
Help us to see that you travel with us on the road of life
and you never leave us.
Fill us with your Spirit,
that we may proclaim the Good News
and tell others of your love.
We remember today all who are suffering because of their faith,
those who live in fear and those whose lives are restricted.

Silence

Lord, abide with us:
stay with us and help us.

We remember before you all travellers
and those who provide transport.
We ask your blessing
upon those who feel they are going into the dark
and to the end of life.
We pray for political prisoners
and the work of Amnesty International.
We remember all who are captive to doubt, fear or sin.

Silence

Lord, abide with us:
stay with us and help us.

Lord, may we be at home with you in our homes.
When our hearts burn within us,
may we know that you are near.
Help us to know you are with us
in all our dealings with others.
We remember today all who are lonely or feel rejected
and all who feel they are missing out on life.

Silence

Lord, abide with us:
stay with us and help us.

We pray for all who have lost vision and hope,
for all who are struggling with life.
We remember the broken-hearted,
those suffering from broken relationships,
all who are broken by illness or trouble,
all who can no longer cope on their own.
Lord, may they know you in their breaking
for you alone can make us whole.

Silence

Lord, abide with us:
stay with us and help us.

Lord as in you we are born anew,
we remember before you the faithful departed.
We rejoice in the fellowship of all your saints.
May we share with them
and all our loved ones, both here and departed,
in the joy and fullness of life eternal.

Silence

Merciful Father,
accept these prayers
for the sake of your Son,
our Saviour Jesus Christ.
Amen.

Fourth Sunday of Easter

YEAR A

Blessed are you, Lord our God,
for in your Son Jesus Christ
you have triumphed over darkness and death
and opened to us the way to eternal life.
Through Christ our Saviour
you have given us new hope and joy.
As we rejoice in his presence
may we give glory to you.
Blessed are you, Father, Son and Holy Spirit.

We give thanks for Jesus the Good Shepherd
and we pray for all who are called
to share in his ministry as shepherds
and guides of your flock.
We pray for all bishops, priests and deacons,
for preachers of the word
and ministers of the sacraments.
We ask your blessing upon all who are involved in pastoral care
and those who seek out the lost and the straying.

Silence

Hear us and help us,
through Jesus Christ our Lord.

Loving God, we pray for all who express your love
in the way they care for others.
We pray for all who are striving for justice
and the relief of poverty.
We remember all social workers, carers and good neighbours.
We ask your blessing
upon all who feel at the mercy of circumstance
and who are unable to manage on their own.

Silence

Hear us and help us,
through Jesus Christ our Lord.

Lord, bless our homes and our loved ones.
May we show respect and care for the world around us
and not be caught up with selfishness and greed.
Help us through our love for each other
to reveal your love in the world.

Silence

Hear us and help us,
through Jesus Christ our Lord.

We give thanks that through Jesus
we can walk with confidence and hope.
We ask your blessing upon all who struggle
in darkness and fear,
all who feel lost
and those who are captives to vice and sin.
We remember friends and loved ones who are ill
and all the struggling people of our world.

Silence

Hear us and help us,
through Jesus Christ our Lord.

We rejoice in the risen Lord and the promise of eternal life.
Lord, bless our loved ones departed.
May they share with your saints in glory.
To you and your unfailing love
we commit ourselves and the whole world
in time and for eternity.

Silence

Merciful Father,
accept these prayers
for the sake of your Son,
our Saviour Jesus Christ.
Amen.

Fifth Sunday of Easter

YEAR A

Blessed are you, Lord God,
for in your Son Jesus Christ
you have opened for us the way to glory.
In him the world is seen in greater depth
and in him is the gift of eternal life.
Lord, ease our troubled hearts
and help us to put our faith in you.
Blessed are you, Father, Son and Holy Spirit.

Lord God, teach us to walk in your way
and to rejoice in your truth,
that we may know the fullness of life eternal.
We ask your blessing upon all spiritual leaders,
preachers of the word and ministers of the sacraments.
We pray for all who are new to the faith
and all who are growing in a deeper awareness of your presence.
May we all know that wherever we go and whatever happens
you are with us and ready to lead us.

Silence

Lord, guide our journeying:
be with us always.

Lord God, we ask your blessing
upon all leaders of nations and peoples.
We pray for your guidance
in the decisions they make this week
concerning the well-being of the world
and of the communities they serve.
We remember before you
all who strive for justice and peace in our world.
We ask for your protection upon all who are seekers or travellers.

Silence

Lord, guide our journeying:
be with us always.

Lord God, we give thanks
for all who have taught us
and guided us into the ways of truth,
those who shared with us their faith and their vision of life.
We ask your blessing upon all schools, colleges and universities.
We pray for our own homes and loved ones
and ask that our homes may show
your abiding presence and love.

Silence

Lord, guide our journeying:
be with us always.

Lord God, we ask your blessing
upon all who feel confused about life
and all who have lost their way.
We pray especially for all who are caught up
in the darkness of despair
and those involved in drugs or vice.
We pray for those who live a lie and cannot face the truth.
Lord, bless all who are suffering from broken relationships
and who are troubled in heart.
We remember all who are ill and fearful for their future.

Silence

Lord, guide our journeying:
be with us always.

Lord God, in your Son you have prepared for us
a place in your kingdom.
Lead us into the fullness of life and joy in your presence.
Bless all our loved ones departed,
that they may rejoice with your saints in glory.

Silence

Merciful Father,
accept these prayers
for the sake of your Son,
our Saviour Jesus Christ.
Amen.

Sixth Sunday of Easter

YEAR A

Blessed are you, Lord our God,
for out of your love you have made all things.
You come to us and give yourself to us.
Help us to be aware of your love in our lives
and to give ourselves to you
in love and in doing your will.
Blessed are you, Father, Son and Holy Spirit.

Lord, as you abide in us,
let our lives show your love for all of your creation.
We remember all Christians
who are being persecuted for their faith
or have to suffer scorn and mockery
from those with whom they live.
We pray for all who witness to you
amid danger and opposition.
We ask your blessing upon all who are new to the faith.
We pray for those who have recently been converted
and for those who have been baptised and confirmed.

Silence

Lord of life,
be known to be among us.

Lord, we remember all places where people are suffering
from tyranny or lawlessness.
We pray for all who are oppressed or used as cheap labour.
We ask your blessing upon all who strive
for justice, freedom, peace and fair trade.

Silence

Lord of life,
be known to be among us.

Lord, may our homes reflect the love we share.
Keep us sensitive to the needs of each other.
May we be ready to take our share
in the work of our own home.
We remember before you
all who feel unloved and unwanted.
We ask your blessing
upon all homeless people and refugees.
We pray for all who are suffering
from broken relationships and broken trust.

Silence

Lord of life,
be known to be among us.

Lord of light, we ask your blessing
upon all who are struggling with darkness and fear.
We remember those who have been involved
in accidents or in acts of violence this week.
We pray for all who have suddenly become ill
and those who are in hospital.
We pray for all who anxiously await
the results of a medical examination.

Silence

Lord of life,
be known to be among us.

Lord of life,
we rejoice in the power of the resurrection
and we remember before you
all your saints and martyrs.
We ask your blessing upon our loved ones and benefactors
who have now departed from us.
May we all abide in your presence and eternal love.

Silence

Merciful Father,
accept these prayers
for the sake of your Son,
our Saviour Jesus Christ.
Amen.

Ascension Day

YEAR A

Blessed are you, Lord our God,
for in the ascension of your Son
you have raised us on high
and given us a glimpse of eternal life
and the promise of your abiding presence.
Blessed are you, Father, Son and Holy Spirit.

Risen and ascended Lord,
you have promised to be with us always.
Help us to rejoice in your presence
and to proclaim your saving power.
We ask your blessing upon all who preach the Good News,
all who teach from the Scriptures
and all who witness to you in their daily lives.

Silence

Ascended Lord, King of kings,
rule in our hearts and in the world.

Risen and ascended Lord,
you are the King of kings.
We pray for the time
when the kingdoms of this world
will be seen as your kingdom.
We ask your blessing upon all rulers,
leaders and politicians,
that they may be guided by your rule.
We pray for all who are in captivity
through injustice or tyranny.

Silence

Ascended Lord, King of kings,
rule in our hearts and in the world.

Risen and ascended Lord,
we rejoice that you are with us
in our homes and our daily lives.
May we be at home with you.
We remember all who live in bad housing,
squalor or deprivation.
We pray for all who have been made homeless
and for any who are suffering
from broken relationships.

Silence

Ascended Lord, King of kings,
rule in our hearts and in the world.

Risen and ascended Lord,
we remember before you all who have lost hope
and have no vision of glory.
We pray for those who live mediocre lives
and all who are caught up in crime, vice or drugs.
We ask your blessing upon all who are ill
and especially those who are nearing death.

Silence

Ascended Lord, King of kings,
rule in our hearts and in the world.

Risen and ascended Lord,
you have opened for us the gate of glory.
We rejoice in the fellowship of your saints
and the faithful departed.
As we ask your blessing
upon our loved ones departed from us,
we commit this world, each other and ourselves
to your unfailing love.

Silence

Merciful Father,
accept these prayers
for the sake of your Son,
our Saviour Jesus Christ.
Amen.

Seventh Sunday of Easter

YEAR A

Blessed are you, Lord our God,
for you have raised your Son
from the darkness of death
to the fullness of life eternal,
to your right hand on high.
By his death he has destroyed death;
by his rising to life again
he has restored to us eternal life;
by his ascension he has opened for us the gate of glory.
Blessed are you, Father, Son and Holy Spirit.

As we rejoice in the ascension,
we give thanks for men and women of vision,
for those who have shared their faith with us.
We remember all whose lives are clouded by doubt or despair.
We pray for those who feel life is dull,
that they may come to know
the joy of the presence of the ascended Lord.
Lord, empower your Church
to proclaim the Good News of your saving acts.

Silence

Lord, with us always,
hear us and help us.

As we rejoice in your presence,
we remember all who feel lonely and neglected in our world.
We ask your blessing on all who are oppressed
and those who are struggling to survive.
We pray for all who are caught up in violence and war,
and for those not at peace with each other,
with themselves and with you.

Silence

Lord, with us always,
hear us and help us.

As we rejoice in your love,
we remember our loved ones,
our homes and families.
We pray for our community and neighbourhood.
We ask your blessing
upon all who strive to brighten the world
by their dedication and goodness,
by their faith and willingness to sacrifice.

Silence

Lord, with us always,
hear us and help us.

As we rejoice in your power,
we remember all whose powers are waning,
the elderly and the infirm
and all who are disabled.
We ask your blessing upon all who are ill
or who have been injured in accidents.
May they find courage and hope in you
and in your abiding love.

Silence

Lord, with us always,
hear us and help us.

We rejoice that you are our great High Priest,
who ascended into heaven,
and that you are at the right hand of God
making intercession for us.
May our loved ones departed and all your faithful
rejoice in you and rest in the glory of your kingdom.

Silence

Merciful Father,
accept these prayers
for the sake of your Son,
our Saviour Jesus Christ.
Amen.

Pentecost

YEAR A

Blessed are you, Lord our God.
To you be praise and glory for ever.
As your Spirit moved over the face of the deep,
bringing life to the world,
and as the same Spirit filled the disciples at Pentecost,
come to us, refresh us and renew us.
Blessed are you, Father, Son and Holy Spirit.

Holy Spirit of God, moving in the deep of creation,
come into the depths of our lives,
guide us and empower us.
We ask your blessing upon the Church,
that it may have the courage
to proclaim the Good News and tell of your power.
May the Church be seen as Spirit-filled
through its display of the gifts of the Spirit.
Guide us, that each of us may use our gifts and talents
to your glory and the benefit of each other.

Silence

Holy Spirit of God, come:
refresh us and renew us.

Holy Spirit of God, giving life to dry bones,
we ask your blessing upon all who feel threatened
or who have lost hope.
We remember before you
refugees, homeless and oppressed peoples.
Give your strength to all who seek to bring liberty and justice.
Guide the leaders of nations
and all who are in positions of authority
into the ways of peace.

Silence

Holy Spirit of God, come:
refresh us and renew us.

Holy Spirit of God, kindle the hearts
which without you are dull and cold.
Bless us in all our relationships,
strengthen our love for each other,
give joy to us as families in our homes
and in our dealings with each other.
We pray for all who seek to restore broken relationships.

Silence

Holy Spirit of God, come:
refresh us and renew us.

Holy Spirit of God, Breath of Life,
we ask your blessing upon all who feel hindered or isolated
through illness or disability.
We remember those in constant pain
and all who are finding life difficult.
We pray for all who are despairing and depressed.

Silence

Holy Spirit of God, come:
refresh us and renew us.

Holy Spirit of God, Giver of life and life eternal,
we rejoice in your renewing and restoring power.
We ask your blessing upon our loved ones departed,
that in you they may know the fullness of life
and the joy of your presence.

Silence

Merciful Father,
accept these prayers
for the sake of your Son,
our Saviour Jesus Christ.
Amen.

Trinity Sunday

YEAR A

Blessed be God, Father, Son and Holy Spirit,
the Three in One,
the holy and wonderful Trinity
bound together in one eternity of love.
Blessed be God the Creator of all things.
Blessed be the Christ, our Saviour and Friend.
Blessed be the Spirit within us, our Guide and Strength.
Blessed be God for all that he is and all he has done.
Blessed be the One and the Three.

Holy God, we ask your blessing
upon all who are baptised and confirmed in the faith,
that they may witness to your presence and love.
We pray for preachers and teachers,
that they may seek to reveal
the mystery of your being with us.
Lord, guide the mission and outreach of your people.

Silence

Holy God, Holy and Strong One,
hear us and help us.

Holy God, we give thanks for your whole creation.
Guide and bless all who work in research
and who seek to discover the mysteries of your world.
We remember all scientists and explorers.
We pray for all who are at school, college or university.
We ask your blessing upon all who provide us
with our daily needs.

Silence

Holy God, Holy and Strong One,
hear us and help us.

Holy God, be among us
in our homes and in our work.
Surround our loved ones and ourselves
with your love and protection.
We ask your blessing upon all who are recently married
and those who have a new child in their family.

Silence

Holy God, Holy and Strong One,
hear us and help us.

Holy God, you are ever ready to help us.
We ask your blessing upon all doctors, nurses
and those caring for loved ones who are ill.
We remember all ill and suffering peoples,
the poor and hungry of our world.
We pray for all who feel they are without help or hope.

Silence

Holy God, Holy and Strong One,
hear us and help us.

Holy God, giver of life and life eternal,
we rejoice in your presence
and ask your blessing upon our loved ones
who are departed from us.
May they share with your saints
in the fullness of your glorious kingdom.

Silence

Merciful Father,
accept these prayers
for the sake of your Son,
our Saviour Jesus Christ.
Amen.

Proper 4

Sunday between 29 May and 4 June inclusive
(if after Trinity Sunday)

YEAR A

Blessed are you, Lord our God.
You are our refuge and strength,
an ever-present help in trouble.
We seek to put our trust in you and to do your will,
that your kingdom may come in us as it is in heaven.
Blessed are you, Father, Son and Holy Spirit.

Lord God, help us to build our lives on a firm foundation:
to put our trust in you and your saving love.
Strengthen your Church when it is beset
by the storms of the world,
that it may remain firm in the faith
and obedient to you.
We pray for all who are seekers,
looking for meaning and purpose in their lives
and in the world.
We remember all who are being persecuted for their faith.

Silence

Lord, your kingdom come,
your will be done.

We ask your blessing upon all who teach and influence others,
upon those who set standards
and offer ways of living to our society.
We pray for all who are involved in government,
in broadcasting and in the press.
We remember all whose lives
have been caught up in floods, famine or war,
all who feel fragile and endangered.
We pray for all who help others to rebuild their lives.

Silence

Lord, your kingdom come,
your will be done.

We give thanks for those who have provided us
with security and protection.
We ask your blessing upon our homes and our loved ones.
We pray for the places where we work
and for those with whom we spend our leisure time.
We remember all homeless and stateless people.

Silence

Lord, your kingdom come,
your will be done.

We bring before you
all whose world has fallen apart this week.
We remember those who have lost loved ones,
who have lost freedom, employment
or who have had their homes repossessed.
We pray for all who have been involved in accidents
or who have suddenly become ill.
We ask your blessing
upon those who are close to death.

Silence

Lord, your kingdom come,
your will be done.

We ask your blessing upon our loved ones
who have departed from us –
passing through that great flood we call death.
May they rejoice in your welcome
and in your kingdom.

Silence

Merciful Father,
accept these prayers
for the sake of your Son,
our Saviour Jesus Christ.
Amen.

Proper 5

Sunday between 5 and 11 June inclusive
(if after Trinity Sunday)

YEAR A

Blessed are you, Lord our God,
for out of your love
you call us to know and to love you.
Lord, may we come to know you,
and in knowing you, love you,
and in loving you, serve you,
whose service is perfect freedom.
Blessed are you, Father, Son and Holy Spirit.

Lord, as you have called us
make us worthy of our calling.
We ask your blessing
upon all who seek to fulfil their calling in life.
We pray for those who are called to proclaim the Gospel
and to give account of you.
We pray for preachers and evangelists.
We ask your guidance
upon all who are called to witness to you,
to your power and your love.

Silence

We come to your love:
heal us and raise us up.

We remember before you all who suffer from rejection and scorn.
We pray for homeless people, for refugees and the world poor.
We ask your blessing upon all who are used as cheap labour
or who are abused by taskmasters.
We pray for all who suffer from injustice
or the lack of fair trade.

Silence

We come to your love:
heal us and raise us up.

We give thanks for our homes and our loved ones.
As we ask your blessing upon them,
we remember homes where there is sorrow and suffering.
We pray for those who are struggling
due to the illness of a loved one,
those who have got deeply into debt
and those who feel drained and exhausted.

Silence

We come to your love:
heal us and raise us up.

We give thanks
for all who work in the healing professions,
and we pray for our own doctors and health workers.
We remember all who are denied healing and help
through poverty or war.
We ask your blessing upon all who are caring
for a loved one who is terminally ill,
and for the work of hospices.

Silence

We come to your love:
heal us and raise us up.

We give thanks for all you have lifted from death
into the fullness of life eternal.
We rejoice with all the faithful departed
who are where sorrow and pain are no more.
To you, to your power and love,
we commit this world,
our loved ones and ourselves
now and for ever.

Silence

Merciful Father,
accept these prayers
for the sake of your Son,
our Saviour Jesus Christ.
Amen.

Proper 6

Sunday between 12 and 18 June inclusive
(if after Trinity Sunday)

YEAR A

Blessed are you, Lord our God,
for you have called us into life and to love you.
You have called us to proclaim your love and power
in all the world.
Lord, send us out in the power of your Spirit,
that we may tell of you and your abiding presence.
Blessed are you, Father, Son and Holy Spirit.

Lord, we ask your blessing upon your Church,
that we may show signs of being One in you,
holy and dedicated to being apostolic
as we reach out to all peoples.
We pray for all who are reaching out to others
in your name and in love.
Bless and guide all who preach the word
and all who share in your healing ministry.
We remember those who work to relieve the distress and sorrow
of people and nations.

Silence

Lord, as you have called us,
hear us and help us.

We pray for all who are called to govern
and all who influence the minds of others.
We pray for leaders of industry
and great multi-national companies and for all they work with.
Lord, help us to show our care for the earth
and our respect for the individual in all that we do.
We remember those whose lives are blighted
by the greed or insensitivity of others.

Silence

Lord, as you have called us,
hear us and help us.

We give thanks because you show us your love
through those who love us.
We ask your blessing upon our homes and our loved ones.
We pray for homes where there is stress and distress.
We remember all who are finding it difficult to cope
and those who are deeply in debt.
We pray for all who are seeking to help those in need.

Silence

Lord, as you have called us,
hear us and help us.

We give thanks for all involved in the healing ministry.
We ask your blessing upon doctors and nurses
and all the emergency services.
We pray for those who are good neighbours and carers
in their local community.
We remember all who are frustrated
through illness or a disability,
and all who are struggling with life.

Silence

Lord, as you have called us,
hear us and help us.

We rejoice in the fellowship of all your saints,
in all who have heard your call and done your will.
We ask your blessing upon our loved ones
who are departed from us.
May we all share in the joy of your love and your kingdom.

Silence

Merciful Father,
accept these prayers
for the sake of your Son,
our Saviour Jesus Christ.
Amen.

Proper 7

Sunday between 19 and 25 June inclusive (if after Trinity Sunday)

YEAR A

Blessed are you, Lord our God,
for you created this world out of your goodness
and pour your love upon it.
All things are precious in your sight
and all are valued.
Blessed are you, Father, Son and Holy Spirit.

God, our Protection and Strength, we bring before you
all who are suffering for their faith,
all who are mocked, scorned, rejected
and in danger.
We remember those imprisoned
and those who suffer physical harm.
We pray for all who seek to proclaim your love
and to help in the healing of nations.
We ask your blessing
upon the Church to which we belong
and pray that we may use aright
the resources you have given us.

Silence

God, in your love and mercy,
hear us and help us.

God our Creator,
we ask you to bless and guide
all who work for the conservation of the earth
and for the care of each creature.
We pray for those involved in the protection
of endangered species
and we pray for those who seek to preserve
the rainforests and their inhabitants.

Silence

God, in your love and mercy,
hear us and help us.

We give thanks for the comfort and security
of our homes.
May we always be aware of the needs of others
and the danger of seeking the cheapest goods.
We ask your blessing upon our families and friends,
that they may know of your love and care.

Silence

God, in your love and mercy,
hear us and help us.

Loving God, we remember in your presence
all whose lives are endangered at this time.
We pray for those who have been involved in accidents
or acts of violence.
We remember those who have been driven off their land
or out of their homes.
We pray for all who are suffering in any way.

Silence

God, in your love and mercy,
hear us and help us.

Lord, you care for us in life and in death
and you offer us life eternal.
We ask you to give joy and peace
to our loved ones departed
and to all your saints.
May we come one day with them
to share in the fullness of your glory.

Silence

Merciful Father,
accept these prayers
for the sake of your Son,
our Saviour Jesus Christ.
Amen.

Proper 8

Sunday between 26 June and 2 July inclusive

YEAR A

Blessed are you, Lord our God,
for you have called us to be your people,
to represent you and to show your love.
By the power of your Spirit
enable us to live and work to your praise and glory.
Blessed are you, Father, Son and Holy Spirit.

We give thanks for all who have gone out in mission
and proclaimed the Good News in word and deed.
We remember especially
those who brought the Gospel to our land.
We ask your blessing upon preachers of the word
and on all who witness to you
by their lifestyle and example.
We pray for all who have never heard the Gospel
and those who are afraid to commit themselves.
We ask you to protect all missionaries who face hostility.

Silence

Loving God,
hear us and help us.

We remember all who live in a hostile environment,
those who are suffering from war or oppression.
We ask your blessing
upon all who seek to bring peace and healing
to the divisions of our world
and all who strive to bring freedom and justice
to nations and individuals.
We remember the work of the United Nations
and Amnesty International.

Silence

Loving God,
hear us and help us.

Father, we thank you for the love of our homes
and ask your blessing upon our families and friends.
We remember all who suffer
from rejection or violence in their homes.
We pray for all who have been taken into care
or those living on the streets of our cities and towns.

Silence

Loving God,
hear us and help us.

Father, we give thanks for your healing love.
We remember before you all suffering people,
the ill and the hungry,
the world poor and the unemployed.
We ask your blessing upon all who are terminally ill
and those who are caring for them.
We pray for helpers who feel exhausted
or who feel they are not appreciated.

Silence

Loving God,
hear us and help us.

We give thanks that, through Christ,
the way to the fullness of your kingdom
is open to us.
We pray for our loved ones departed.
We commend them to you
as we do the world and ourselves.

Silence

Merciful Father,
accept these prayers
for the sake of your Son,
our Saviour Jesus Christ.
Amen.

Proper 9

Sunday between 3 and 9 July inclusive

YEAR A

Blessed are you, Lord our God,
for you are a very present help in trouble.
You are more ready to hear than we to pray,
and willing to give us more than we desire or deserve.
We come to you for rest, for renewal,
for the strength to do what you would have us do.
Blessed are you, Father, Son and Holy Spirit.

We give thanks for the Church throughout the world.
We remember today all who are weary in their service
and all who are in danger of losing faith.
We pray for priests and pastors
who are working in difficult areas and with little support.
We ask your blessing
upon all who are seeking to share the burdens
of those with great responsibilities.
We pray for all who are carers
and who are giving support to others.

Silence

Lord, we come to you:
renew us and give us peace.

As we rejoice in the gift of life,
we remember the world-weary,
the overwrought and the anxious.
We pray for all who are laden with troubles or guilt.
We ask your blessing upon all who are overworked or oppressed
and those who are fearful for the future.
We remember those who have lost the joy of living
and all who cannot easily relax.

Silence

Lord, we come to you:
renew us and give us peace.

We give thanks for our friends and loved ones,
for those who share our joys and our sorrows.
We remember all who have been a support
and comfort to us.
We pray for families where there is tension and stress
and we remember all who feel lonely and without help.

Silence

Lord, we come to you:
renew us and give us peace.

We give thanks, O Lord, for continual support
and we pray for all who feel uncared for or unwanted.
We remember all who are at the point of breaking
and all those who have broken down.
We ask your blessing upon all who are ill
and are finding life difficult.
We pray for all who seek to be a help and a support.

Silence

Lord, we come to you:
renew us and give us peace.

We ask your blessing
upon all who have found their rest in you.
We remember our friends and loved ones departed.
May they find in you rest, renewal
and the joy of the resurrection.

Silence

Merciful Father,
accept these prayers
for the sake of your Son,
our Saviour Jesus Christ.
Amen.

Proper 10

Sunday between 10 and 16 July inclusive

YEAR A

Blessed are you, Lord our God,
for you come to us
and seek to make your home with us.
Let our doors and our ears be open to you.
Let our hearts find their rest and their joy in you,
that we may grow in grace and live to your glory.
Blessed are you, Father, Son and Holy Spirit.

We ask your blessing upon all who proclaim the Good News.
We pray for preachers and evangelists,
for teachers in schools and Sunday schools.
We remember all at theological colleges.
May we hear and receive your word,
that it may grow in us and that we may serve you.
We pray for all who have never heard
or who have closed their minds to the Gospel.

Silence

Loving God,
hear us and help us.

We give thanks for the harvests of our world
and for all who provide us with food and our needs.
We pray for farmers and all who work in agriculture.
We ask your blessing upon all who suffer from a bad harvest.
We remember the world poor and the hungry.
We ask your guidance upon all who work for Fair Trade.

Silence

Loving God,
hear us and help us.

We give thanks for our homes
and pray that you will always be at home
in our homes and our hearts.
We pray for the young who are growing in the faith
and for their nurture.
May we all make room
in our lives and in our days
to know you and your love.
We remember all who are struggling
with their relationships
and pray for all who have hardened their hearts.

Silence

Loving God,
hear us and help us.

We ask your guidance upon all who are caught up
in the cares of this world,
who are over-wrought and anxious.
We remember those who are fearful of what the future holds,
for all who are lost in materialism
and know no standards but those of wealth.
We pray for all who have become poor in spirit.
We ask your blessing upon all who are ill or suffering
and their loved ones who care for them.

Silence

Loving God,
hear us and help us.

We give thanks for your saints in glory
and pray that our loved ones departed
may know the joy of your kingdom.
We commend this world, our families and ourselves
to your unfailing love.

Silence

Merciful Father,
accept these prayers
for the sake of your Son,
our Saviour Jesus Christ.
Amen.

Proper 11

Sunday between 17 and 23 July inclusive

YEAR A

Blessed are you, Lord our God,
for you have given us a world full of beauty and wonder
and have created us in your image.
Yet we have abused the world and marred your image.
Lord, in your goodness, heal your world and restore us.
Blessed are you, Father, Son and Holy Spirit.

We give thanks
that you have called us to work for you.
Through your Spirit
give us the gifts of wisdom and love in all our dealings.
We ask your blessing upon the Church
where it is working among the oppressed
and rejected peoples of our world.
Give your Church courage to stand against evil
and work for the good of all.

Silence

Lord, guide us
and help us.

We give thanks
for the balance and harmony of your creation.
We pray for all who are working to stop pollution
of land, sea and air;
all who work to protect
the species and the harvests of our world.
We ask your blessing upon those
who seek to care for the rain forests.
We pray for all who strive for justice
and for the social welfare of all people.

Silence

Lord, guide us
and help us.

We give thanks
for our loved ones and our homes
and ask you to bless and protect us.
We remember all who are forced to live
in slums or shantytowns
and those who live on the streets of our cities.
We pray for all whose relationships have broken down,
especially those full of anger or guilt.

Silence

Lord, guide us
and help us.

We pray for all who have suffered
through the wickedness or evil of others.
We remember victims of crime, violence and abuse.
We pray for all whose memories are scarred.
We ask your blessing on households that have suffered
because one member has gone astray.
We pray for all who are ill and in need of care.

Silence

Lord, guide us
and help us.

We give thanks that you are a loving and forgiving God;
in you we can be healed, restored and renewed.
We ask you to bless our loved ones departed,
that they may know and rejoice in your love.
We commit ourselves and all of creation
to your saving power and love.

Silence

Merciful Father,
accept these prayers
for the sake of your Son,
our Saviour Jesus Christ.
Amen.

Proper 12

Sunday between 24 and 30 July inclusive

YEAR A

Blessed are you, Lord our God,
for you have given us of your kingdom.
You invite us to share in your godly rule
and in the riches of life that is eternal.
Lord, teach us to seek you
until we know you and love you
and are aware of your transforming power in all the world.
Blessed are you, Father, Son and Holy Spirit.

We ask your blessing upon all who seek
to proclaim the Good News of your kingdom.
We pray for preachers of the word
and ministers of the sacraments,
for evangelists and all who witness in their daily lives
to your presence and power.
We remember those who quietly transform their surroundings
for the better
and those who show others of your kingdom in their midst.

Silence

Lord, your kingdom come,
in us as it is in heaven.

Lord we ask for the gift of discernment
in those who influence the lives of others.
We pray for all who are involved in shaping our world
through government,
through broadcasting and the press.
We ask your blessing upon all who teach
and all who are set up as examples
for our young people to follow.

Silence

Lord, your kingdom come,
in us as it is in heaven.

We give thanks for the great riches you have given us
through our home and loved ones.
May we always appreciate the care and attention
that have been shown to us.
As we have richly received, so may we share;
as we are loved, so may we love.
We pray for homes where there is tension
and a breakdown in relationships.

Silence

Lord, your kingdom come,
in us as it is in heaven.

May we not lose sight of things eternal
among all that happens in our lives.
We ask your blessing upon all who find life dull,
all who are depressed or have lost hope.
We pray for all who struggle with illness
or difficult circumstances.
We remember those who are in hospital
and all who cannot cope on their own.

Silence

Lord, your kingdom come,
in us as it is in heaven.

We give thanks for the promise
of your kingdom and life eternal.
We rejoice in the fellowship of all your saints
and commend our loved ones departed,
this world and ourselves
to your unfailing love.

Silence

Merciful Father,
accept these prayers
for the sake of your Son,
our Saviour Jesus Christ.
Amen.

Proper 13

Sunday between 31 July and 6 August inclusive

YEAR A

Blessed are you, Lord our God,
for you provide food for our daily needs
and for all creatures.
You give food, resources and talents
for us to share with others and give you glory.
Blessed are you, Father, Son and Holy Spirit.

We ask your blessing
upon all who hunger and thirst
for righteousness and the coming of your kingdom.
We remember all who feel their lives are parched and dry
and who suffer from spiritual hunger.
May the Good News be brought to all
who feel empty and that life is meaningless.
We bring before you all who go out in mission
and all who seek to proclaim your love.

Silence

Renewing and refreshing God,
hear us and help us.

We ask your blessing
upon all who lack the necessary resources for well-being.
We pray for all who are suffering
from hunger and poverty,
all who struggle due to injustice and greed.
We remember all who have lost crops and livestock
through famine, drought or war.
We pray for the work of Christian Aid
and for all who seek to bring relief
to the hungry and poor.

Silence

Renewing and refreshing God,
hear us and help us.

We give thanks for our loved ones,
for all who have cared and provided for us.
We ask your blessing upon all who work
to give us what we need.
We pray for all farmers and food providers,
for shop workers
and all who bring our food to the markets.
We ask your blessing upon our families
and our neighbours.

Silence

Renewing and refreshing God,
hear us and help us.

We remember all who feel weary with life,
drained of energy and no longer able to cope.
We pray for all who struggle against great odds.
We ask your blessing upon all who feel alone
and that no one cares for them.
We pray for all who are ill at home or in hospital.

Silence

Renewing and refreshing God,
hear us and help us.

We give thanks that you give life and life eternal,
that you are a renewing and restoring God.
As we rejoice in the resurrection,
we ask your blessing upon our loved ones departed.
May they know the peace and glory of your kingdom.

Silence

Merciful Father,
accept these prayers
for the sake of your Son,
our Saviour Jesus Christ.
Amen.

Proper 14

Sunday between 7 and 13 August inclusive

YEAR A

Blessed are you, Lord our God,
for you are a very present help in trouble.
You are ready to hear our cry
and come to our aid.
Lord, help us not to be afraid
but to put our trust and hope in you.
May we ever rejoice in your love and care.
Blessed are you, Father, Son and Holy Spirit,
one God for ever.

Lord, you have created us out of love
and for your love.
We ask for your protection
in the troubles and storms of life.
Bless all Christians who are struggling against great odds.
We pray for those who are suffering
from persecution, violence or ridicule.
We remember those whose lives are at risk
and those who are exhausted.

Silence

Lord, in the storms of life,
hear us and help us.

We give thanks for the work of the Mission to Seafarers
and those who go out in lifeboats.
We pray for all whose work is upon the sea.
We ask your blessing upon fishermen,
merchant seamen and the Royal Navy.
We remember today all who are caught up
in storms, in earthquakes, floods or droughts.

Silence

Lord, in the storms of life,
hear us and help us.

We give you thanks
for the safety and protection of our homes.
We pray for all who are struggling
with problems of debt
or whose relationships are breaking down.
We pray for the work of Shelter
and remember all who are homeless
and living on the streets of our towns and cities.

Silence

Lord, in the storms of life,
hear us and help us.

Lord, we pray for your blessing
upon the world-weary, the worried and worn,
all who feel overwhelmed and unable to cope.
We remember all who are ill at home or in hospital
and those who care for them.
We pray especially for any involved in accidents
or whose illness finds no cure.

Silence

Lord, in the storms of life,
hear us and help us.

Lord, stand by us when the last great storm
seeks to overwhelm us
and we feel we are sinking beneath the waves.
Help us to know that in you we will not perish
but have everlasting life.
To you we commit all our loved ones departed:
may they rejoice in your presence and in your peace.

Silence

Merciful Father,
accept these prayers
for the sake of your Son,
our Saviour Jesus Christ.
Amen.

Proper 15

Sunday between 14 and 20 August inclusive

YEAR A

Blessed are you, Lord our God,
for you have created us all out of love
and for your love.
Even when in our sin and foolishness
we go against you and leave you,
you are there and seek us out in love.
Blessed are you, Father, Son and Holy Spirit.

Loving God, may your Church throughout the world
show your love for all peoples and nations.
Bless all who seek to heal divisions
and to do away with prejudice.
Give courage to all who reach out to those in need
and who seek to welcome the rejected.
May your Church reflect your saving love.

Silence

Lord of life and love,
hear us and help us.

Loving God, we ask forgiveness
for the sin and arrogance that divides us
and creates barriers between nations and peoples.
We pray with love for all minority groups,
for those who are judged by their race,
colour or history.
We remember all who are refugees, homeless
or outcasts of society.
We ask your blessing upon all who work
to bring a new unity and understanding
between divided peoples.

Silence

Lord of life and love,
hear us and help us.

Loving God, we thank you for our homes
and for all who have accepted us
in love and generosity.
We ask your blessing upon our homes
and the community in which we live.
We pray for all who are suffering from broken relationships
and all who feel estranged from the world around them.

Silence

Lord of life and love,
hear us and help us.

Loving God, we give thanks for our health and well-being.
We ask your blessing upon all who are ill
at home or in hospital.
We remember today all who suffer
from autism or schizophrenia
and all who are mentally ill.
We ask your blessing upon all
who are separated from their loved ones through illness
and all who feel rejected.

Silence

Lord of life and love,
hear us and help us.

Loving God, in your redeeming love
you accept us and welcome us.
We ask you to give joy and peace
to all our loved ones who have departed this life:
may they know the fullness of salvation.
To you and your love we commit the whole world,
our loved ones and ourselves.

Silence

Merciful Father,
accept these prayers
for the sake of your Son,
our Saviour Jesus Christ.
Amen.

Proper 16

Sunday between 21 and 27 August inclusive

YEAR A

Blessed are you, Lord our God,
for in your love you sent your Son Jesus Christ
to be our Saviour.
You deliver us from the darkness of sin and death
and open to us the way to eternal life.
Blessed are you, Father, Son and Holy Spirit.
To you be praise and glory for ever.

We give thanks for all who have witnessed
to your love and saving power.
We ask your blessing upon all preachers of the word
and ministers of the sacraments,
that they may keep us aware of your presence
and wonderful power.
We pray for all who are growing in the faith,
and all who attend study groups and Bible class.
We pray especially today
for all who are struggling with their faith
and those who have fallen away.

Silence

Jesus, Saviour of the world,
we look to you to save and help us.

We give thanks for the wonders of creation
and the mystery of life.
We ask your blessing upon all who suffer
from injustice, war or violence.
We remember those caught up in natural disasters
and struggle due to famine or flood.
We pray for those who feel life has no purpose or meaning
and all who are tempted to despair.

Silence

Jesus, Saviour of the world,
we look to you to save and help us.

We give thanks for the love of our homes and dear ones,
for all the help and encouragement they have given us.
We ask your blessing on homes were life is restricted
and where there is little joy.
We remember all who are homeless, all who are deeply in debt
and all who are uncertain of their future.

Silence

Jesus, Saviour of the world,
we look to you to save and help us.

We give thanks for all who share in your healing
and bringing of peace to peoples and nations.
We ask your blessing upon all who are struggling
against evil or with illness.
We remember especially
those for whom life brings little joy or hope.
We pray for friends and loved ones who are ill
and all who feel lonely or frightened at this time.

Silence

Jesus, Saviour of the world,
we look to you to save and help us.

We give thanks that through Christ
we are offered eternal life.
We ask your blessing upon all your saints
and our loved ones departed.
We commend them, this world and ourselves
to your unfailing love.

Silence

Merciful Father,
accept these prayers
for the sake of your Son,
our Saviour Jesus Christ.
Amen.

Proper 17

Sunday between 28 August and 3 September inclusive

YEAR A

Blessed are you, Lord our God,
for in your Son you have come among us
and shared in our humanity,
that we may come to you and share in your divinity.
You have given us a wonderful Saviour
and revealed the depth of your love.
Blessed are you, Father, Son and Holy Spirit.

Lord God, we seek to do your will,
that your Church may be the instrument
of your peace and salvation.
We ask your blessing upon all who go out in mission
and all who proclaim the Good News.
We remember especially
any who risk their lives or well-being
for the sake of doing your will.
We pray for all who seek to dedicate their lives
to you and your glory.

Silence

Lord, your will be done
on earth as in heaven.

Lord God, may your will be done
on earth as it is in heaven.
We ask your blessing upon all
who strive to bring healing and wholeness
to peoples and nations.
We pray for peacekeeping forces
and all who endeavour to maintain law and order.
We pray for the United Nations
and for our queen and government.

Silence

Lord, your will be done
on earth as in heaven.

Lord God, may we reveal your will in our homes
by living together in love and peace.
We ask your blessing upon our loved ones and friends.
May we encourage one another to do your will.
We pray for all who suffer from bad housing
or live in areas of deprivation.
We ask your blessing
upon all who seek to relieve the needs of the poor.

Silence

Lord, your will be done
on earth as in heaven.

Lord God, we pray today for all who are suffering
from strained or broken relationships.
We remember all who are a bad influence
and lead others astray.
We pray for all caught up in drugs or vice.
May they be given the chance of new directions.
We pray for friends and loved ones who are ill or in trouble.

Silence

Lord, your will be done
on earth as in heaven.

Lord God, we give thanks for our salvation
through Jesus Christ our Saviour.
Bless your saints and our loved ones departed
with the joy of your presence
and the fullness of life eternal.

Silence

Merciful Father,
accept these prayers
for the sake of your Son,
our Saviour Jesus Christ.
Amen.

Proper 18

Sunday between 4 and 10 September inclusive

YEAR A

Blessed are you, Lord our God,
for you accept us in our sin,
you forgive all who are penitent
and give us the opportunity of newness of life.
Blessed are you, Father, Son and Holy Spirit.

Loving and forgiving God,
we rejoice in your presence
and we remember before you
all who seek to build up your Church in love.
We ask your blessing upon all who are being prepared
for baptism or confirmation.
We pray for all who seek forgiveness
and want to start afresh.

Silence

Forgiving God,
hear us and help us.

Loving and forgiving God,
we remember in your presence
all who work for reconciliation
between peoples and nations.
We pray for all who seek to heal old hurts
and historical grievances.
Bless all peacemakers
and all who work to bring unity and understanding
within communities.
We pray for the work of the United Nations
and all who seek to bring justice and fair dealings
to our world.

Silence

Forgiving God,
hear us and help us.

Loving and forgiving God,
may our homes reflect your love.
Forgive our petty divisions and jealousies,
our quarrelling and our anger.
Lord, through our homes and loved ones
teach us forgiveness, tolerance and compassion.
May our homes and our community
be seen as caring and loving.

Silence

Forgiving God,
hear us and help us.

Loving and forgiving God,
we remember in your presence
all whose lives are spoiled by hatred
and the desire for revenge.
We pray for all who feel they cannot be forgiven
and who cannot forgive.
We ask your blessing
upon all who are troubled in mind or spirit
and all who are tempted to give up hope.

Silence

Forgiving God,
hear us and help us.

Loving and forgiving God, we give thanks
that we are ransomed, healed, forgiven.
We ask your blessing
upon our friends and loved ones departed,
that knowing your forgiveness
they may rejoice in your love.

Silence

Merciful Father,
accept these prayers
for the sake of your Son,
our Saviour Jesus Christ.
Amen.

Proper 19

Sunday between 11 and 17 September inclusive

YEAR A

Blessed are you, Lord our God,
for you have revealed your love and forgiveness
through your Son Jesus Christ.
Through him we are ransomed, healed and forgiven.
As we have freely received,
may we freely give.
Blessed are you, Father, Son and Holy Spirit.

God of mercy, we come to you for forgiveness and renewal.
We ask you to bless all who are seeking to change their lives
and live to serve others and to glorify you.
Though we are unworthy
we seek your acceptance of us.
May your Church reveal your love
in its care for all who come to it.
We pray today for prison chaplains and clergy
who work in areas of crime and vice.

Silence

Lord, forgive our sins
and heal our infirmities.

God of mercy, we ask your blessing
upon the poor, hungry and homeless of the world,
and all migrant and displaced peoples.
We remember nations that are in great debt
and the work of the world banks and governments
to relieve this debt.
We pray for all who are bankrupt
and all who have lost the little that they had.
We bring before you all who are fearful for their future.

Silence

Lord, forgive our sins
and heal our infirmities.

God of mercy, you have given to us richly;
may we richly give.
Let us not hoard or squander
the good things you have given us.
Let us help those in need and use our gifts to your glory.
We ask your blessing upon our homes
and upon all who have enriched our lives
by their goodness and love.

Silence

Lord, forgive our sins
and heal our infirmities.

God of mercy, we pray
for all who have become hard-hearted,
all who are unable to forgive and all who seek revenge.
Through your love may they find a change of attitude and heart.
We ask your blessing upon all who are abused,
all who are used as cheap labour
and all who do not receive a fair wage.
We bring before you friends and loved ones who are ill.

Silence

Lord, forgive our sins
and heal our infirmities.

God of mercy, we give thanks
for all who have witnessed to your love and generosity.
We rejoice in the fellowship of the saints.
We commend our loved ones departed,
this world and ourselves
to your unfailing love and mercy.

Silence

Merciful Father,
accept these prayers
for the sake of your Son,
our Saviour Jesus Christ.
Amen.

Proper 20

Sunday between 18 and 24 September inclusive

YEAR A

Blessed are you, Lord our God,
for you have given us a good earth
and a wonderful life.
May we use the resources of the earth aright
to respect all of creation,
relieve the needs of the poor
and give you glory.
Blessed are you, Father, Son and Holy Spirit.

Creating and loving God,
we thank you for the beauty and balance of our world.
We give glory to you for the mystery and wonders of creation.
May your Church help to witness
that the world belongs to you.
We pray for all who seek to proclaim the Good News
in areas of deprivation or opposition.
We ask your blessing upon all who preach the word
and all who do so by their example.

Silence

Gracious God, in your goodness,
hear us and help us.

Creating and loving God,
we ask you to bless with wisdom
all who are employers
and all who direct multinational companies.
May they not abuse or treat their workforce with injustice.
We pray for all who seek to bring about fair trade.
We remember also all who are unemployed
or do not have enough resources for healthy living.

Silence

Gracious God, in your goodness,
hear us and help us.

Creating and loving God,
we thank you for our homes and loved ones.
Help us to respect all who work
to supply us with our needs.
We pray for all who work
in the farming and retail industries.
May we always be aware that all good comes from you.
We ask your blessing upon all who are homeless
and all who feel they are not loved.

Silence

Gracious God, in your goodness,
hear us and help us.

Creating and loving God,
we remember all ill and suffering people.
We pray for those who are struggling to survive
and all who are oppressed by war, violence and tyranny.
We ask your blessing upon all who have been injured
or who have suffered from acts of violence.

Silence

Gracious God, in your goodness,
hear us and help us.

Creating and loving God,
you give us all that we have
and you offer us life eternal.
We rejoice in the fellowship of all your saints
and we commend our loved ones departed,
the whole of your creation and ourselves
to your unfailing love.

Silence

Merciful Father,
accept these prayers
for the sake of your Son,
our Saviour Jesus Christ.
Amen.

Proper 21

Sunday between 25 September and 1 October inclusive

YEAR A

Blessed are you, God our Father,
for you have sent your Son to be our Saviour.
In him you have delivered us
from the dominion of darkness
and made us children of the day and of light.
Blessed are you, Father, Son and Holy Spirit.

Loving Father, we give you thanks
for the coming of our Lord Jesus Christ
for in him you have opened the gate to eternal life.
Bless all who seek to proclaim the Good News,
all who preach the word and go out in mission.
We remember all who witness in their daily life
and all who seek to serve you faithfully.

Silence

Holy God, holy and strong One,
hear us and help us.

Loving Father, we ask your blessing
upon all who have important decisions to make this week.
We pray for those who are rulers and politicians,
for scientists and research workers,
for judges and all who strive to bring peace.
We remember all who find it hard to remain faithful and loyal
and pray that they may be given new strength and courage.

Silence

Holy God, holy and strong One,
hear us and help us.

Loving Father, we give thanks
for our homes and our loved ones.
We pray for all who have influenced our lives
through their example and teaching.
We remember all families
where relationships are breaking down
or life has become hard.
We ask your blessing
upon those who have to make difficult decisions
about their homes, their relationships or their way of life.

Silence

Holy God, holy and strong One,
hear us and help us.

Loving Father, we remember all
who are confused by the many choices in life
and who find it hard to cope.
We pray for those who have lost their freedom
and all who suffer from tyranny.
We ask your blessing upon all who are ill
and those who have decided they need to go into care.

Silence

Holy God, holy and strong One,
hear us and help us.

Loving Father, we thank you
that Jesus came down to lift us up
into the fullness of your kingdom.
We rejoice in the fellowship of your saints in glory.
We remember before you
all our friends and loved ones departed.
We commit our lives and all of your creation
to your unfailing love.

Silence

Merciful Father,
accept these prayers
for the sake of your Son,
our Saviour Jesus Christ.
Amen.

Proper 22

Sunday between 2 and 8 October inclusive

YEAR A

Blessed are you, Lord our God,
for you are our Creator
and you have called us to know you
and proclaim your love.
Help us to be aware that you speak to us through the Scriptures
and through those who tell of your presence and power today.
Blessed are you, Father, Son and Holy Spirit.

Father Creator, raise up among us
prophets and preachers
who will tell of your mighty acts and your saving power.
To scientists and research workers
give vision of the wonder and mystery of your world.
Bless your Church with an awareness of
and living relationship with Christ,
that it may witness to the power of the resurrection.
We pray for all Christians who are suffering
from persecution or rejection.

Silence

Lord and Saviour of all,
hear us and help us.

Father Creator, we ask your blessing
upon leaders of peoples
and all who influence our lives by their decisions.
Give them wisdom and respect in all their dealings.
We pray for all who work in the field of genetics
and those who influence our world by their actions.
We remember all who seek to show us
how to care for the world.

Silence

Lord and Saviour of all,
hear us and help us.

Father Creator, we give thanks
for our homes and our loved ones.
We ask your blessing upon all homes
where there is tension and misunderstanding.
We pray for marriages that are struggling
and families that are in danger of falling apart.
We remember all who feel rejected or neglected.

Silence

Lord and Saviour of all,
hear us and help us.

Father Creator, we give thanks
for all you have given to us.
We pray for the world poor, the oppressed
and all who are suffering from violence.
We remember those who have been driven off their own land
and all who are refugees.
We ask your blessing upon all who are ill
or who have been injured
and all who are fearful for their future.

Silence

Lord and Saviour of all,
hear us and help us.

Father Creator, we give thanks
for Jesus Christ the living Lord
and for the power of his resurrection.
We commit to your keeping our loved ones departed,
that they may rejoice in the fullness of your kingdom,
and we pray that we may share with them
in the knowledge of your love.

Silence

Merciful Father,
accept these prayers
for the sake of your Son,
our Saviour Jesus Christ.
Amen.

Proper 23

Sunday between 9 and 15 October inclusive

YEAR A

Blessed are you, Lord our God,
for you have called us
to know you and to love you.
You invite us to experience the joy
of coming into your presence
and to delight in your grace.
Lord, we come
depending on your grace and goodness.
Blessed are you, Father, Son and Holy Spirit.

Good and gracious God,
may our lives show the joy of knowing you and your love.
Let preachers and teachers encourage all who hear them
to come to you in love.
Bless all who seek to extend our lives
by a vision of your grace and goodness.
We pray today for all religious writers and broadcasters.

Silence

Lord of life and love,
grant us the joy of your kingdom.

Good and gracious God,
as we go about our daily work
may we show our joy in your presence.
We ask your blessing upon all who encourage us
to relax, to be still and to be attentive.
We pray for artists and musicians,
for craftspeople and gardeners,
for all who beautify our world.
We remember all who live in deprived and derelict areas
and pray especially for the world poor.

Silence

Lord of life and love,
grant us the joy of your kingdom.

Good and gracious God,
we thank you for the love and attention
we have received through our homes and dear ones.
We ask your blessing upon our families and friends
and the communities in which we live and work.
We remember all who strive to improve our environment.
We pray for all who are homeless
and those who live on the streets
of our towns and cities.

Silence

Lord of life and love,
grant us the joy of your kingdom.

Good and gracious God,
we thank you for our well-being.
We ask your blessing upon all who are sad or depressed
and all whose lives are darkened with troubles.
We remember all who are ill
and their loved ones as they care for them.
We pray for those who work in hospitals
and all who care for people in trouble.

Silence

Lord of life and love,
grant us the joy of your kingdom.

Good and gracious God,
you invite us all into your presence,
and to life eternal.
May we not lose sight of the eternal
through the clamour and call of the world.
We ask your blessing upon our loved ones departed.
May they rejoice with the saints in the fullness of eternal life.

Silence

Merciful Father,
accept these prayers
for the sake of your Son,
our Saviour Jesus Christ.
Amen.

Proper 24

Sunday between 16 and 22 October inclusive

YEAR A

Blessed are you, Lord our God.
All things come from you
and of your own do we give you.
From you come our life, this world
and all that we have and are.
Teach us to love and respect your creation
and give glory to you.
Blessed are you, Father, Son and Holy Spirit.

Lord God, Creator of all, we give thanks
for those who have taught us the faith.
We ask your blessing upon the mission of the Church,
which is your mission.
Guide and strengthen all who reach out to others
in faith and with the Good News.
We pray for all evangelists
and all who witness to your love.

Silence

Lord God, Maker of heaven and earth,
in your love hear us.

Lord God, Creator of all, we give thanks
for all you have given us.
We ask your guidance on all who are led astray
by the glitter of gold
and the false promises of consumerism.
We pray for all who are impoverished in spirit.
We ask your blessing
upon the governments of the world
and their striving for justice and fair dealing.

Silence

Lord God, Maker of heaven and earth,
in your love hear us.

Lord God, Creator of all, we ask your blessing
upon our home and our loved ones.
We pray for all who provide us
with water, electricity and gas,
for those who collect our refuse and clean our streets.
We remember all who help to maintain law and order.

Silence

Lord God, Maker of heaven and earth,
in your love hear us.

Lord God, Creator of all, we ask your blessing
upon all hospitals, care homes,
home visitors and the social services.
We remember before you
all suffering and impoverished peoples.
We pray for the world poor
and all who are without the basic needs of life.
We bring before you friends and loved ones who are ill.

Silence

Lord God, Maker of heaven and earth,
in your love hear us.

Lord God, Creator of all, we come from you
and we return to you.
Bless our loved ones departed.
May they rejoice with your saints in glory.
We commit this world and ourselves
to you and your unfailing love.

Silence

Merciful Father,
accept these prayers
for the sake of your Son,
our Saviour Jesus Christ.
Amen.

Proper 25

Sunday between 23 and 29 October inclusive

YEAR A

Blessed are you, Lord our God,
for you love us with an everlasting love.
We rejoice that nothing can separate us
from your love in Christ Jesus.
Lord, help us to show your love to each other
at all times.
Blessed are you, Father, Son and Holy Spirit.

Loving God, we give thanks
for the fellowship of the Church
and for all who have taught us the faith.
We pray for preachers and teachers,
for evangelists and Bible translators.
We ask your blessing upon all Sunday schools,
study groups and those who are learning to pray.
We remember all who are seeking to grow
in love of you and in faith.

Silence

God of love,
hear us and help us.

Loving God, we give thanks
for all who reveal your love and care
through dedicated lives.
We ask your blessing upon all those who work
among the deprived and under-privileged peoples
of the world.
We remember all who seek to bring peace and unity
to communities and nations.
We pray for all who are homeless and in need.

Silence

God of love,
hear us and help us.

Loving God, we give thanks
for all who have shown us love and care.
We ask your blessing upon our homes and loved ones.
We remember all who are separated from their loved ones
through illness or circumstance.
We pray especially for the lonely
and any who feel unloved.

Silence

God of love,
hear us and help us.

Loving God, we thank you
for all who reveal love
through working in the healing professions.
We pray for doctors and nurses
and remember our own doctors and hospitals.
We ask your blessing upon all who are ill or suffering,
especially those who have no one to care for them.

Silence

God of love,
hear us and help us.

Loving God, we give you thanks
for the gift of eternal life.
We rejoice in the fellowship of all your saints
and ask your blessing upon all our loved ones departed.
May we share with them
in the fullness and glory of your kingdom.

Silence

Merciful Father,
accept these prayers
for the sake of your Son,
our Saviour Jesus Christ.
Amen.

All Saints' Day

1 November or Sunday between 30 October and 5 November inclusive

YEAR A

Blessed are you, Lord our God,
for you have called us to share
in the blessedness of your saints.
Grant that in the darkness that is around us
we may be guided by their example
and so serve you in love and peace.
Blessed are you, Father, Son and Holy Spirit.

Rejoicing in the fellowship of all the saints
we pray to the Lord:

Lord, make us to be numbered with your saints
in your eternal glory.

Blessed God, we remember before you
all who have witnessed to your love and mercy.
We ask your blessing
upon all who seek to bring reconciliation and forgiveness
to peoples and communities.
We pray for all who are involved in pastoral work
and the ministry of healing.

Silence

Lord, make us to be numbered with your saints
in your eternal glory.

Blessed God, we remember before you
all who have witnessed to your peace.
We ask your blessing upon the work of the United Nations
and all peacekeeping forces.
We pray for all who are not at peace
with themselves or with the world around them
and all who suffer through war.

Silence

Lord, make us to be numbered with your saints
in your eternal glory.

Blessed God, we remember before you
all who have set us an example by their grace and goodness.
We ask your blessing upon our homes and families.
We pray for all who are suffering from broken relationships
and all who feel lonely.

Silence

Lord, make us to be numbered with your saints
in your eternal glory.

Blessed God, we remember before you
all who have suffered persecution for their faith.
We ask you to bless those who strive against injustice and evil.
We pray for all who suffer from tyranny or oppression.
We remember also all who are ill at home or in hospital,
those injured in accidents and all victims of violence.

Silence

Lord, make us to be numbered with your saints
in your eternal glory.

Blessed God, we remember before you
all the faithful departed.
We pray that our loved ones who are gone from us
may rejoice in the fellowship of all your saints in glory.

Silence

Merciful Father,
accept these prayers
for the sake of your Son,
our Saviour Jesus Christ.
Amen.

Fourth Sunday before Advent

Sunday between 30 October and 5 November inclusive; for use if the Feast of All Saints was celebrated on 1 November and alternative propers are needed

YEAR A

Blessed are you, Lord our God,
for amidst the trials and troubles of the world
you are present and ready to help us.
You sent your Son
so that we should not perish
but have eternal life.
Blessed are you, Father, Son and Holy Spirit.

We give thanks to you, O Lord,
for the Church
and the hope that it brings to troubled lives.
We ask your blessing upon Christians
who are being persecuted for their faith
or who risk their lives in the care of others.
We remember all relief agencies
and those who work in war-torn areas,
in areas of earthquake or famine.

Silence

Lord, we put our trust in you:
hear us and help us.

We give thanks, O Lord,
for all who seek to bring peace and harmony to our world.
We ask your blessing upon leaders of nations
and all peacekeeping forces.
We pray especially
for those whose lives are endangered at this time.

Silence

Lord, we put our trust in you:
hear us and help us.

We give thanks, O Lord,
for our homes and our loved ones.
We ask your blessing
upon all who have been driven out of their homes
through acts of violence, natural disaster or debt.
We pray for those who find they can no longer cope
in their own home.

Silence

Lord, we put our trust in you:
hear us and help us.

We give thanks, O Lord,
for the healing services.
We pray for all doctors and nurses,
for paramedics and those who work in ambulances
or rescue vehicles.
We ask your blessing upon all whose world has fallen apart
through sickness or loss of a loved one.

Silence

Lord, we put our trust in you:
hear us and help us.

We give thanks, O Lord,
for the gift of eternal life.
We rejoice in the fellowship of all your saints
and ask your blessing upon our loved ones departed.
May we all share with you in the fullness of your kingdom.

Silence

Merciful Father,
accept these prayers
for the sake of your Son,
our Saviour Jesus Christ.
Amen.

Third Sunday before Advent

YEAR A

Blessed are you, Lord our God,
for you come to us and abide with us always.
Your light scatters the darkness from before us
and you invite us to let this shine through us
and reveal you to the world.
In your love help us to be children of light.
Blessed are you, Father, Son and Holy Spirit.

Lord of light and love,
we ask your blessing upon the Church
throughout the world.
We pray especially for areas
where the faith has grown dim
and vision has been lost.
We remember all who are struggling
against dark and evil forces.
We pray for all who seek
to bring the light of Christ to others.

Silence

Lord of light,
awaken us to your presence.

Lord of light and love,
strengthen all who are on their guard against evil
and seek to bring peace and harmony to our world.
We remember before you
all who are suffering
through oppression or violence,
all who are used as cheap labour
and all who are without proper homes or enough food.
Bless all who work tirelessly for their relief.

Silence

Lord of light,
awaken us to your presence.

Lord of light and love,
make us alert to your presence with us and in our homes.
Bless and protect our families and our friends.
Make us alert to the needs of our community,
where we can help and be of use.
Let us not miss opportunities of showing your love.

Silence

Lord of light,
awaken us to your presence.

Lord of light and love,
bless all whose lives are darkened by illness or tragedy.
We remember all who feel afraid
and those who regret work undone
or doing what they should not have done.
We pray for all who are terminally ill
and all who can no longer look after themselves.

Silence

Lord of light,
awaken us to your presence.

Lord of light and love,
we ask your blessing upon all our friends and loved ones
who are departed from us.
May they rejoice in your light and love
in your kingdom.
We pray for all your saints
and all who have reflected your light in the world.

Silence

Merciful Father,
accept these prayers
for the sake of your Son,
our Saviour Jesus Christ.
Amen.

Second Sunday before Advent

Sunday between 13 and 19 November inclusive

YEAR A

Blessed are you, Lord our God,
for you have given us all talents and abilities.
You have created each of us in a unique way,
that we may give our own unique service and talents to you.
Blessed are you, Father, Son and Holy Spirit.

Lord, giver of all good gifts,
we give you thanks for all you have given us.
May we share our talents and use them
to the benefit of others and for your glory.
We pray today for all who tell others of your love
and proclaim the Gospel.
We ask your blessing upon all who minister to others.

Silence

Giver of all good gifts,
hear us and help us to live to your glory.

Lord, giver of all good gifts,
we ask your blessing upon all artists, musicians, craftspeople,
gardeners, architects, politicians
and all who use their gifts to improve our world.
We remember all who are unable to use their talents to the full
through oppression or other circumstance.

Silence

Giver of all good gifts,
hear us and help us to live to your glory.

Lord, giver of all good gifts, bless us and our loved ones.
We pray that our homes may be places where talent is fostered
and given the chance to grow.
We ask your blessing upon all schools and places of learning
and all who help others to develop skills.

Silence

Giver of all good gifts,
hear us and help us to live to your glory.

Lord, giver of all good gifts,
bless all who are thwarted in their ability
through illness, oppression or the lack of opportunity.
We pray for all who are struggling
due to poverty and hunger.
We remember before you loved ones and friends who are ill.

Silence

Giver of all good gifts,
hear us and help us to live to your glory.

Lord, giver of all good gifts,
we thank you for the gift of life eternal.
We rejoice in the fellowship of all your saints
and ask your blessing on our loved ones departed,
that they may be at home with you
in your kingdom of love.

Silence

Merciful Father,
accept these prayers
for the sake of your Son,
our Saviour Jesus Christ.
Amen.

Christ the King

Sunday between 20 and 26 November inclusive

YEAR A

Blessed are you, Lord our King and our God,
for you have made us and we belong to you.
You have revealed your love for us
in the coming of Christ our Lord
and in the sending of the Holy Spirit.
Blessed are you, Father, Son and Holy Spirit.

Loving Lord, we ask your blessing
upon all who seek to care for your people.
We pray for all bishops, priests and deacons,
all who preach the word, administer the sacraments
and show pastoral care.
May we all share in your outreach and mission of love.
We remember especially those who are reaching out
to the confused and the lost.

Silence

King of Love,
Good Shepherd, hear us.

Loving Lord, we ask your blessing
upon this world, which is your creation.
We remember today all who are struggling
against evil, war or poverty.
We pray for all who share in your redeeming work
through their caring for others
and seeking to bring them freedom.
We pray for all relief agencies
and all who reach out to those in need.

Silence

King of Love,
Good Shepherd, hear us.

Loving Lord, we ask your blessing
upon our homes and our loved ones.
We remember today all who live alone
and those who are homeless.
We pray especially for young people
living on the streets of our towns and cities
and all whose lives were diminished
by circumstances they could not avoid.

Silence

King of Love,
Good Shepherd, hear us.

Loving Lord, we ask your blessing
upon all who are ill at home or in hospital.
We remember also loved ones
who are caring for them
and are anxious and fearful.
We pray for all who cannot cope on their own.
We ask your blessing upon all carers
and those involved in medical care
and the rescue services.

Silence

King of Love,
Good Shepherd, hear us.

Loving Lord, we ask your blessing
upon our friends and loved ones
who have departed from us.
May they share with your saints in glory.
To you and your loving presence
we commit this world and ourselves
and ask that we may know you
as the King of Love, our Saviour and our Friend.

Silence

Merciful Father,
accept these prayers
for the sake of your Son,
our Saviour Jesus Christ.
Amen.

Year B

First Sunday of Advent

YEAR B

As we begin another Church Year
let us give thanks to God that he has made us,
that he loves us and that he comes to us.

O God, you are our Maker:
you give us life, you give us love,
you give us yourself.
Help us to give our lives, our love and ourselves to you.
Keep us alert and aware of your presence,
that we may meet you each day
and know that you come to us in grace and in love.

Lord, as you come to your Church,
help us to reveal your glory.
Grant that we may show your grace
and your goodness in our lives.
We thank you for the grace and goodness
revealed in Jesus Christ
and that we are enriched in him.

We remember churches that are struggling
against the darkness of evil, of opposition, of apathy.
We remember especially
Christians who are being persecuted for their faith.

Silence

Come, Lord Jesus;
come, our Saviour and our God.

As we pray for your world,
we remember those who are seeking
to bring peace and goodwill among all.
We pray for those involved in war or the threat of war.
We think of those caught up in earthquakes, famine or flood.

Silence

Come, Lord Jesus;
come, our Saviour and our God.

Lord, let your presence be known in our homes and our actions.
May people be thankful for us
and our care of all that is around us.
We pray that you will show yourself to us
through our loved ones and friends.

Silence

Come, Lord Jesus;
come, our Saviour and our God.

We remember all whose lives are darkened by pain and distress;
all who are struggling with doubt and despair;
all whose faith is shaken by what is happening around them.
We pray for members of our community and friends
who are ill at this time.

Silence

Come, Lord Jesus;
come, our Saviour and our God.

God our Father, your grace has been given to us,
in the gift of eternal life and in your abiding presence.
We pray for all who are departed from us,
for friends and loved ones
in the fullness of your eternal kingdom.
We rejoice with them in the gift of life and your love.

Silence

Merciful Father,
accept these prayers
for the sake of your Son,
our Saviour Jesus Christ.
Amen.

Second Sunday of Advent

YEAR B

We pray that we and your whole Church
may be prepared for your coming to us.
When you come
may you find us a holy and a godly people;
may you find us striving for peace
and looking forward to your glory.

Silence

Lord, change us:
and we shall be changed.

We remember today all who are being baptised.
We pray for the parents and the godparents.
We come with all who are sorry for their sins
and want to lead a new life;
with all who seek forgiveness and cleansing.

Silence

Lord, change us:
and we shall be changed.

We remember all who are striving for peace.
Bless the leaders of nations and peacekeeping forces.
Guide the United Nations and the work of relief agencies.
May we strive for justice and freedom for all peoples.

Silence

Lord, change us:
and we shall be changed.

Lord, we ask that our homes
may be places of welcome, love and harmony.
May we make room for you in our lives and our work.

Silence

Lord, change us:
and we shall be changed.

We come before you with all who are struggling:
those who are ill at home or in hospital;
the world poor, the oppressed
and all who suffer from violence or rejection.
We ask that we may know your healing presence.

Silence

Lord, change us:
and we shall be changed.

And we remember before you all who have died,
our friends and loved ones departed
and all your saints.

Silence

Merciful Father,
accept these prayers
for the sake of your Son,
our Saviour Jesus Christ.
Amen.

Third Sunday of Advent

YEAR B

Eternal light shine in our hearts,
that our days may be bright with your presence.
May we be aware
of the great things that you have done for us
and rejoice in your salvation.

We remember all who walk in darkness
and do not know the love of God.
We remember those who have never heard the Good News.
We pray that the whole Church may reach out
in mission, in service and in love.
We pray especially for the Church
where it has lost vision or sense of outreach.

Silence

Eternal light,
shine in our hearts.

Remember our world where people are oppressed;
where there is hunger and poverty.
We ask you to strengthen all who work for peace
and to relieve the poor.
At this time we pray especially for . . .
May we do all that we can to help.

Silence

Eternal light,
shine in our hearts.

We give you thanks for our homes and our loved ones,
for the freedom and the peace that is ours.
May we be sensitive to the needs of those around us
and be of help when we can.

Silence

Eternal light,
shine in our hearts.

God give strength and courage to all who are ill,
to those involved in accidents or acts of violence.
We remember those who have lost their freedom
or their homes.
We pray especially for . . .
We give thanks for all who work in hospitals
and for our own doctors.

Silence

Eternal light,
shine in our hearts.

We rejoice that you have freed us
from the slavery of sin and death
and brought us to the glorious liberty
of the children of God.
We rejoice in the gift of eternal life,
and pray for friends and loved ones departed.

Silence

Merciful Father,
accept these prayers
for the sake of your Son,
our Saviour Jesus Christ.
Amen.

Fourth Sunday of Advent
YEAR B

O God, as we prepare for Christmas
may we be ready for your coming to us.
As we make space for friends and relatives
may we make room in our lives for you.
In our daily living let us seek to do your will
and help to bring in your kingdom.

Through the working of the Church,
through obedience to you,
through reaching out in mission,
through the proclaiming of the Gospel,
your kingdom come:
your will be done.

Through our striving for peace,
through our caring for the poor,
through our desire for justice,
through the ways we seek to improve your world,
your kingdom come:
your will be done.

Through our love in our homes,
through our honesty and sensitivity,
through our relationships and friends,
through our hopes and our ambitions,
your kingdom come:
your will be done.

Through the healing of the ill,
through looking after the lonely,
through our compassion and care,
your kingdom come:
your will be done.

We remember especially today
any who have asked for our prayers
or who are in trouble or danger.
We ask that we may share with them
in the fullness of your kingdom.

Silence

Merciful Father,
accept these prayers
for the sake of your Son,
our Saviour Jesus Christ.
Amen.

Christmas Day

YEAR B

Father, we rejoice and sing,
for you love us with a great love.
We give thanks to you for the coming of our Lord Jesus Christ
into our world and into our lives.
Let us enjoy your presence with us,
and the love you offer to us in Jesus our Lord.

We give thanks for all who celebrate Christmas,
all who are worshipping in churches and in their homes,
all who acknowledge Jesus in their midst.

Bless the outreach and the mission of your Church.
Give all your people the courage to tell the Gospel story
and proclaim your presence and love.

We remember all whose lives are darkened by fear,
those who have no faith,
those who doubt God and themselves.

Silence

Jesus, Light of the World,
come scatter the darkness.

We ask for peace on the earth
and good will among all peoples,
that we may learn to accept your peace,
share your peace and live your peace.
We remember before you
all who suffer from war or violence at this time,
especially . . .

Silence

Jesus, Light of the World,
come scatter the darkness.

We give thanks for our homes
and the friends with whom we will celebrate this Christmas.
We remember absent friends and loved ones.
We remember all who are lonely
or feel rejected at this time.

Silence

Jesus, Light of the World,
come scatter the darkness.

We remember in your presence
all who are ill at home or in hospital,
all who are struggling in any way.
We pray for doctors and nurses
and everyone who will have to be at work today.

Silence

Jesus, Light of the World,
come scatter the darkness.

We give thanks that Jesus came down to lift us up,
that he lived that we might not die.
We remember loved ones departed
in the fullness of your kingdom.

Silence

Merciful Father,
accept these prayers
for the sake of your Son,
our Saviour Jesus Christ.
Amen.

First Sunday of Christmas

YEAR B

Lord God, we thank you for the gift of sight
and for the deeper sight
that lets us see you at work in your world.
We pray that our vision may not be impaired
but that we may see you more clearly
and love you more dearly day by day.

We give thanks for the Church throughout the world
and the telling of the Good News.
We pray for all evangelists and preachers,
for pastors and ministers,
for all who have the care of your people.
Teach us to ponder on their words
and treasure them in our hearts.

Silence

May we see you more clearly
and love you more dearly.

We remember all who work to provide us
with food and shelter.
We pray for shepherds and farmers,
for all food producers.
We remember all who work in shops and factories.

Silence

May we see you more clearly
and love you more dearly.

We thank you for our homes and our loved ones.
We remember those who taught us the faith.
We pray for our teachers
and all who have been an example to us.

Silence

May we see you more clearly
and love you more dearly.

We remember today all whose sight is impaired.
We pray for all who have lost vision or hope in the world,
all who feel lonely,
all who have lost a sense of wonder.
We pray especially for those who are ill
at home or in hospital.

Silence

May we see you more clearly
and love you more dearly.

We ask that we may have a vision of your presence
and of your eternal kingdom.
We pray for our loved ones
who have passed from our sight.

Silence

Merciful Father,
accept these prayers
for the sake of your Son,
our Saviour Jesus Christ.
Amen.

Second Sunday of Christmas

YEAR B

Blessed are you, Lord, God of all creation.
The whole universe belongs to you
and yet you care for each one of us.
You come to us in love to be our Saviour and our friend.
You have chosen us to be your people
and given us of your Holy Spirit
We give you thanks and praise.

We share with all who continue to give thanks
for the coming of Jesus into the world.
We remember before you those who proclaim the Gospel
by living lives of holiness and goodness.
We pray for those preparing for Confirmation
and all who are seeking to know you better.

Silence

Let us praise the name of the Lord.
His name only is exalted.

We bring before you rulers of people,
politicians and leaders of nations.
We remember all who are striving
to bring peace and unity to humankind.
We think especially today of rescue workers,
of ambulance workers and firefighters.

Silence

Let us praise the name of the Lord.
His name only is exalted.

We give thanks that you care for us as our Father
and that we all belong to your family.
We pray for our own parents, families and friends.
May we know that you are with us and love us.

Silence

Let us praise the name of the Lord.
His name only is exalted.

You are our Redeemer and are with us in our troubles.
We remember all whose lives are endangered at this time,
all who are fearful and anxious.
We pray to you for those who are ill at home or in hospital.
We trust in your love and power.

Silence

Let us praise the name of the Lord.
His name only is exalted.

You save us from destruction
and have chosen us to be one with you in your kingdom.
We ask you to bless our loved ones departed
with your love and grace.

Silence

Merciful Father,
accept these prayers
for the sake of your Son,
our Saviour Jesus Christ.
Amen.

The Epiphany

YEAR B

God, we give thanks to you
for your love towards all peoples of the world.
You have chosen to give yourself to us all
and invite us to give ourselves to you.
Blessed are you, Lord God, for all things come from you
and of your own do we give you.
We come in our poverty to your riches,
in our foolishness to your wisdom,
in our sorrows to your healing and joy.

Silence

Light of Christ,
shine in our lives.

As we remember the wise men,
we pray for the rich and the comfortable,
all who have plenty of this world's good things.
May they know that all things come from you
and their lives are a gift from you.
May the riches of the world be put to good use.
We remember the world's poor,
the homeless and the hungry.

Silence

Light of Christ,
shine in our lives.

We pray for all who are seekers,
who search for the truth,
who look for meaning and who desire to know you.
We pray for pilgrim peoples,
especially those on their way to Bethlehem or Jerusalem.
We pray for those who are new to our church or community.

Silence

Light of Christ,
shine in our lives.

We give thanks for all who come to you in worship,
all who are aware of awe or mystery in their lives.
We pray for leaders of worship, choirs and organists,
for all who give us a sense of wonder and beauty.

Silence

Light of Christ,
shine in our lives.

We come with all who are in pain or sorrow.
We remember those whose sickness finds no cure,
those who are permanently ill
and those with a short time to live.
We pray for doctors and nurses
and all who are involved in healing.

Silence

Light of Christ,
shine in our lives.

Lord, we worship and adore you.
We offer you our joys and sorrows,
our sickness and health,
our riches and our poverty.
We remember all who have enriched our lives
by their goodness.
We pray for loved ones who are now in the fullness
of your kingdom.

Silence

Merciful Father,
accept these prayers
for the sake of your Son,
our Saviour Jesus Christ.
Amen.

First Sunday of Epiphany
The Baptism of Christ

YEAR B

We rejoice in your presence and your love,
Father, Son and Holy Spirit.
You have made us, you have redeemed us,
and you guide us.
We remember in your presence
all who are being prepared for baptism or confirmation:
all who are seeking to know the gifts of the Spirit.
We pray for our own clergy
and for all who are being prepared
for ordination and ministry.

Silence

God ever with us:
hear us, Father, Son and Holy Spirit.

We pray for all who are starting new work or new studies,
for the newly married and the newly engaged,
for all who are testing their vocations.
We pray for all who seek to bring peace to our world.

Silence

God ever with us:
hear us, Father, Son and Holy Spirit.

We give thanks for our homes and our loved ones,
for our godparents and our godchildren.
We ask your blessing upon them.
We remember all who come from broken homes
or who are suffering from broken relationships.

Silence

God ever with us:
hear us, Father, Son and Holy Spirit.

We pray for all who feel they have lost their way,
who are troubled and distressed,
that they may know your love and care.
We remember also those who are ill at home or in hospital,
all who are struggling at this time.

Silence

God ever with us:
hear us, Father, Son and Holy Spirit.

We praise you for giving us life and life eternal.
We remember especially today
friends and loved ones who have enriched our lives
but who are now departed from this world.
We commend all to you, Father, Son and Holy Spirit.

Silence

Merciful Father,
accept these prayers
for the sake of your Son,
our Saviour Jesus Christ.
Amen.

Second Sunday of Epiphany

YEAR B

Blessed are you, Lord God, Creator of all life.
We thank you because we are wonderfully made.
You have given us the gift of communication,
eyes to see, ears to hear and lips to speak.
Teach us not only to speak to you but to listen,
to be quiet in your presence
and know that you are God.

Silence

Lord, hear us:
graciously hear us.

We pray for all who listen to you in prayer
that they may speak to us of your word.
We ask your blessing upon the leaders of our churches,
upon pastors and counsellors,
upon all who are called to listen
to the needs and troubles of others.

Silence

Lord, hear us:
graciously hear us.

Guide the leaders of the nations
in the ways of justice and peace.
Keep our ears open to the cry of the poor and the oppressed;
let us always be sensitive to the needs of others.
We pray for relief agencies
and all who are working to relieve suffering.

Silence

Lord, hear us:
graciously hear us.

Lord, in our homes help us to listen to each other
with undivided attention.
Teach us to be sensitive to the various calls for us
to share and to care for each other.
We ask you to protect our homes and loved ones.

Silence

Lord, hear us:
graciously hear us.

We remember before you all whose voices are unheard,
people who feel neglected or unwanted.
We pray for the lonely and those who have no helpers.
We remember also all who are ill at this time
at home or in hospital.

Silence

Lord, hear us:
graciously hear us.

We rejoice that you hear us and offer us eternal life.
We pray for our loved ones departed
and for all who have served you faithfully on earth.

Silence

Merciful Father,
accept these prayers
for the sake of your Son,
our Saviour Jesus Christ.
Amen.

Third Sunday of Epiphany

YEAR B

You, O Lord, are almighty, endless in power and in love.
When we have no power to help ourselves
help us to know we can trust in you,
in your presence and in your power.

We pray for the Church
that it may know its true resources and power are from you;
that it may be enabled
to proclaim your saving power and your love.
Give your Church the ability
to be a healing instrument in the world,
to bring peace, and to proclaim your presence.

Silence

Almighty God,
we know all power comes from you.

We remember all who struggle for survival,
the poor and the oppressed, the hungry and the homeless,
all who feel powerless.
We ask you to bless all
who strive to bring justice and peace to our world.

Silence

Almighty God,
we know all power comes from you.

We give thanks for all who have enriched our lives
by their love and goodness.
We ask that your love may be experienced in our homes
and among our loved ones and friends.
We pray for homes where there is conflict,
violence or abuse,
especially for any who live in fear or feel unable to change.

Silence

Almighty God,
we know all power comes from you.

Give strength to the weak,
refresh the weary,
encourage the fearful
and protect all who are endangered.
We remember friends and loved ones
who are ill or in need of comfort and refreshment.

Silence

Almighty God,
we know all power comes from you.

We rejoice that you give us life in all its abundance
and life eternal.
We pray for all our loved ones departed
that they may have the fullness of life in your kingdom.

Silence

Merciful Father,
accept these prayers
for the sake of your Son,
our Saviour Jesus Christ.
Amen.

Fourth Sunday of Epiphany

YEAR B

Gracious God,
you give us a glimpse of your glory
in the face of Jesus Christ.
Through him we are able to come before your presence
and to rejoice in your love.
Through him alone we are counted worthy to approach you.

We give you thanks and praise
for the coming of Jesus into our world.

Silence

Lord of all power and might,
hear our prayer.

We remember in your presence
all who have not heard the Good News.
We pray for those
who do not know anything of being healed or forgiven.
Grant that the Church may proclaim
your love and saving power.
We pray for all who administer the sacraments
and who preach the word.

Silence

Lord of all power and might,
hear our prayer.

We pray for areas of our world
where darkness seems to triumph over light.
We remember people who are possessed by drug addiction.
We remember also those who feel that they are possessed by evil.
May they all come to know the glorious liberty
of the children of God.

Silence

Lord of all power and might,
hear our prayer.

We give you thanks and praise
for those who have shared their faith with us,
for all who have encouraged us in the way of goodness.
We ask your blessing upon them
and upon our loved ones and friends.

Silence

Lord of all power and might,
hear our prayer.

We pray for all who have been ill for a long time,
for those whose illness finds no cure.
We pray for all
who feel they are losing their faculties or mobility,
all who cannot cope on their own.
We remember those who are in hospices.

Silence

Lord of all power and might,
hear our prayer.

We rejoice in the fellowship of the saints.
We remember loved ones who are departed from us.
We commend the whole of creation and ourselves
to your unfailing love.

Silence

Merciful Father,
accept these prayers
for the sake of your Son,
our Saviour Jesus Christ.
Amen.

The Presentation of Christ

YEAR B

Blessed are you Lord our God,
Creator of light and life.
We rejoice in your presence
and seek to live fully in your light.

By the word that created light out of darkness,
grant that your light may shine in your Church.
Let our lives be filled with your light
that others may be drawn to your light.
Let the Church throughout the world
be radiant with your light and love.

Silence

Light of Christ,
shine upon us.

By the light that has come into the world,
reveal your peace and justice to the nations.
Lord, guide our rulers and thinkers
that we may live in harmony and generosity,
that none may hunger or suffer from want.

Silence

Light of Christ,
shine upon us.

By the light that shines in the face of Jesus Christ,
fill our homes with your love and joy.
Bless our families and friends
and all whom we meet.

Silence

Light of Christ,
shine upon us.

By the light that destroys darkness,
bring hope and comfort to all who suffer,
all who are ill at home or in hospital.
We remember all whose lives are darkened
by fear or their past.

Silence

Light of Christ,
shine upon us.

By the light that conquers death,
give to your saints and all the faithful departed
the fullness of life and joy in your eternal kingdom.

Silence

Merciful Father,
accept these prayers
for the sake of your Son,
our Saviour Jesus Christ.
Amen.

Proper 1

Sunday between 3 and 9 February inclusive
(if earlier than the Second Sunday before Lent)

YEAR B

Blessed are you, Lord God Almighty.
You are the giver of life and power;
all energy, all strength comes from you.
We come to you for renewal and refreshment.
We come to rest in your presence
that we may find strength and hope in you.

We pray for all who preach the word
and administer the sacraments,
that they may find great strength from your presence.
May the Church be a place of stillness and refreshment.
May your people show
that you give joy and peace to their lives.

Silence

Lord God, we wait before you.
Renew our strength.

We pray for all who are responsible
for the limited resources of our world,
that we may use them with respect and care.
We ask your blessing
on all who provide our homes with power and light:
those who work in the oil, gas and electric industries.
We remember all who are in emerging nations
and are looking to new sources of power.

Silence

Lord God, we wait before you.
Renew our strength.

We pray for all who expend their energies
in caring for us and loving us.
We ask you to bless our homes and our loved ones.
We pray for those who have taught us
and all who have provided for our needs.

Silence

Lord God, we wait before you.
Renew our strength.

Father, all-powerful,
we remember the needs of the weary,
the powerless, the ill.
We ask your blessing on all who feel
that they cannot cope with life
or who are drained of their resources.
We pray especially for those who are terminally ill.

Silence

Lord God, we wait before you.
Renew our strength.

Father, you are the giver of life and life eternal.
We remember in your presence
the holy ones who have served you.
We pray for our loved ones departed,
that all may be renewed by your power.

Silence

Merciful Father,
accept these prayers
for the sake of your Son,
our Saviour Jesus Christ.
Amen.

Proper 2

Sunday between 10 and 16 February inclusive
(if earlier than the Second Sunday before Lent)

YEAR B

Blessed are you, Lord our God.
You love every one of us and reach out to help us.
We are ever in your care and under your protection.

We come as a divided Church,
often full of mistrust and rejection.
We do not find it easy to accept the sinful
or to forgive our hurts.
We often carry a history of hurts and resentment.
Wholesome God, we come for healing and guidance.

Silence

Let your presence
bring us wholeness and hope.

We come as part of a world
where there is much violence and hatred.
People live in fear of each other
or are at war with each other.
There are many homeless and rejected people.
We pray especially for those with leprosy or AIDS.

Silence

Let your presence
bring us wholeness and hope.

We rejoice in your love and the love of our families.
We remember all lonely people,
all who feel rejected,
all who cannot cope on their own.
Lord, make our community
a loving and caring community.

Silence

Let your presence
bring us wholeness and hope.

We remember all who are isolated through illness.
We pray for those who are in hospital or in a home
and who have no visitors.
We remember those from our own community
who are ill at home or in hospital.

Silence

Let your presence
bring us wholeness and hope.

We rejoice that in you all ills come to an end
and all pain is taken away.
We give thanks for the gift of eternal life.
We give thanks for all the saints
and we remember loved ones who are departed from us.

Silence

Merciful Father,
accept these prayers
for the sake of your Son,
our Saviour Jesus Christ.
Amen.

Proper 3

Sunday between 17 and 23 February inclusive
(if earlier than the Second Sunday before Lent)

YEAR B

Blessed are you, Lord our God.
You forgive us our sins and cleanse us from all iniquity.
You give us the chance to start every day anew.

Lord, may your Church be an accepting and loving Church.
May it help to free those who are paralysed by fear and doubt.
May it reach out to those who do not know of your love
and bring them to you.
We remember we are part of your mission
and we pray for all who are involved in outreach.

Silence

Holy and strong one,
let us rejoice in your saving power.

We remember in your presence
all who are struggling to survive.
We pray for those suffering from drought or flood,
all who are underfed or homeless.
Bless all who work for the relief of the poor and troubled.
We remember the work of Christian Aid, the Red Cross
and all who are good neighbours.

Silence

Holy and strong one,
let us rejoice in your saving power.

We give you thanks for our friends and family,
especially for those who brought us to know you.
We pray for all who teach in our church
and all who set an example of care and love in our community.

Silence

Holy and strong one,
let us rejoice in your saving power.

Lord, let your presence bring comfort to the suffering;
may they know your love and care.
We remember all who are paralysed
or suffering from strokes,
all who are unable to move about freely
and all who are housebound.

Silence

Holy and strong one,
let us rejoice in your saving power.

We give thanks for the power of the resurrection,
and that you offer us life eternal.
We remember all who have lost loved ones this week
and we pray for our loved ones departed.

Silence

Merciful Father,
accept these prayers
for the sake of your Son,
our Saviour Jesus Christ.
Amen.

Second Sunday before Lent
YEAR B

Blessed are you Father, Son and Holy Spirit.
You have made us
and in you we live and move and have our being.
In you we rejoice.
In you is the fullness of life.

We give thanks for the wonders and the beauty of creation.
May we delight in your world as you delight in it.
May your Church show a great love and care for the world –
as you love and care for it.
We pray for all who do not know
of your love or your presence.
We ask you to bless all who preach the word.

Silence

Lord of love,
in you we live and move and have our being.

We pray for all who teach us
to respect and love your world.
Bless all who work in conservation
and in protecting the resources of the earth.
Help us to enjoy the world and delight in it
with artists and musicians and all craftspeople.

Silence

Lord of love,
in you we live and move and have our being.

God, we thank you for your presence
in our homes and communities,
in our schools and in our work.
Bless our loved ones
and all who have enriched our lives by their goodness.

Silence

Lord of love,
in you we live and move and have our being.

God, we ask your presence to bring comfort and hope
to all who are struggling at this time.
We remember those injured in accidents or acts of violence,
those who are ill
and all who are in hospital.

Silence

Lord of love,
in you we live and move and have our being.

You give life and light;
in you life and light are eternal.
May all our loved ones departed and all the saints
rejoice in the fullness of eternal light and love.

Silence

Merciful Father,
accept these prayers
for the sake of your Son,
our Saviour Jesus Christ.
Amen.

Sunday before Lent

YEAR B

Blessed are you Lord God our Father.
You have revealed your hidden glory
in the face of our Lord Jesus Christ;
in Christ you have given us the hope of life eternal.

Bless your Church, O Lord,
with the radiance of your presence.
In each place of worship may we bow before your glory.
We ask you to transform with your brightness
all those places where worship appears to be dull or lifeless.
Fill all preachers and teachers
with a vision of your glory.

Silence

Glorious God,
give us a glimpse of your glory.

Lord of light, transform the dark places of the world
by your presence.
We remember all who live in slums and shantytowns,
all who live among war and dereliction.
Let the radiance of your presence
bring hope to their lives.

Silence

Glorious God,
give us a glimpse of your glory.

Glorious God, fill our homes with your love
and our lives with your glory.
Be with us and all our loved ones
and deliver us from darkness.

Silence

Glorious God,
give us a glimpse of your glory.

We remember all who suffer,
all who are in hospital,
all who are lonely and feel rejected,
all whose lives are in a dark cloud.
We think of those who are fearful of the future
and those whose lives are full of sadness.
Lord, may the light of your love transform their lives.

Silence

Glorious God,
give us a glimpse of your glory.

Give us a glimpse of your glory
and awareness of your gift of eternal life.
As we rejoice in the fellowship of all your saints,
grant to our loved ones departed
the joy and glory of your kingdom.

Silence

Merciful Father,
accept these prayers
for the sake of your Son,
our Saviour Jesus Christ.
Amen.

First Sunday of Lent

YEAR B

Blessed are you, Lord God, Creator of the universe.
You have given us this world to enjoy
and so that we may work in harmony with you.
You have given us talents and abilities
that we may enrich each other.
Blessed are you, Lord God.

Lord, you bless your Church with great riches,
with people of talent,
with a variety of gifts.
Help us to use them aright to your glory
and for the benefit of all.
We remember especially all who lead us in worship
and who teach us the faith.

Silence

Show us your ways, O Lord,
and teach us your paths.

Gracious God,
what a wonderful world you have given us.
We ask your blessing upon all who work the land
and who provide food for us.
We remember all who are working in conservation
and in caring for people in desolate or spoiled areas.

Silence

Show us your ways, O Lord,
and teach us your paths.

We thank you for the comfort of our homes
and the gifts you have given
to each member of our families and loved ones.
Help us to be aware of each other's needs
and the needs of those who are not as well off as we are.

Silence

Show us your ways, O Lord,
and teach us your paths.

Lord, you are always ready to help us in our troubles.
We bring before you
the sorrows and sighing of our world.
We remember all who are ill,
all injured in accidents or acts of violence,
all who are hungry or homeless.
We ask your blessing upon each one
and on all who care for them.

Silence

Show us your ways, O Lord,
and teach us your paths.

We praise you for the gift of eternal life.
We pray for all our loved ones who are departed from us
and are now rejoicing in the fullness of your kingdom.

Silence

Merciful Father,
accept these prayers
for the sake of your Son,
our Saviour Jesus Christ.
Amen.

Second Sunday of Lent

YEAR B

Blessed are you, Lord God.
You have called us into life,
to love and serve you.
You have promised that you are with us always
and that you are our Helper and our Guide.

We give thanks for all who hear and obey your call:
for men and women who willingly sacrifice
and deprive themselves for the good of others.
We remember all who have spent their lives in your service.
We ask you to give strength to all who are quietly seeking
to give you their love and their lives.
We remember today all who suffer rejection, pain or distress
for following you.

Silence

Lord, as you have called us,
hear us when we call upon you.

We remember with gratitude
all who have given their lives in research and exploration
for the good of others.
We ask you to bless all scientists, technicians
and leaders of people.
We pray for those working among the poor
and the deprived of our world.

Silence

Lord, as you have called us,
hear us when we call upon you.

We give thanks for all our parents and loved ones do for us,
for their love, their sacrifice and their care.
We seek your blessing upon our homes and our families.
We remember all who have no one to care for them.

Silence

Lord, as you have called us,
hear us when we call upon you.

We give thanks for the dedication of doctors
and nurses and hospital staff.
We ask your blessing on all who are in hospital
or who are ill at this time
and upon all who look after them.
We remember all who feel that no one cares about them.

Silence

Lord, as you have called us,
hear us when we call upon you.

We rejoice that you have called us to eternal life
and that you have invited us
to enjoy your presence for ever.
We pray for all who have given their lives
in the service of others,
and for our loved ones departed.
May they now rejoice in the fullness of your kingdom.

Silence

Merciful Father,
accept these prayers
for the sake of your Son,
our Saviour Jesus Christ.
Amen.

Third Sunday of Lent

YEAR B

Blessed are you, Lord our God, Creator of the world,
bringing all out of chaos.
We thank you for the guidance of the Scriptures
and for the Commandments.
We remember all who influence the lives of others
through their example or through the media.
We pray that young people
may be given good guidance as they grow,
that they may move with confidence and freedom.
In its rules may the Church show love and compassion,
and that rules are for our freedom and not to restrict life.
May all who teach and preach lead us
towards the glorious freedom of the children of God.

Silence

Lord, your kingdom come,
your will be done.

We look for the time when the kingdoms of this world
will be the kingdom of God.
We long for the time when God's rule
will be what guides us all.
We remember all who are suffering from injustice –
people robbed of their homes or their living.
We pray for native people being driven off their land
due to the greed of others.

Silence

Lord, your kingdom come,
your will be done.

Teach us, Lord, to live in love and harmony with those around us.
Let there be peace in our dealings, in our homes and in our hearts.
May we never oppress or hurt anyone through word or deed.

Silence

Lord, your kingdom come,
your will be done.

We are sorry for all the harm done to the earth
by the greed and the insensitivity
of powerful groups or individuals.
We pray for all who seek to clean up our rivers
and the air we breathe,
all who work in conservation.
We remember before you all who are ill
or in trouble at this time.

Silence

Lord, your kingdom come,
your will be done.

We give thanks that you are ever with us
and offer us life eternal.
We remember friends and loved ones departed from us.
May they rejoice with your saints in glory.

Silence

Merciful Father,
accept these prayers
for the sake of your Son,
our Saviour Jesus Christ.
Amen.

Fourth Sunday of Lent

Mothering Sunday

YEAR B

Blessed are you, Lord God of all creation.
You have loved us from the beginning
when you gave us life through our parents.
You have showered blessings upon us
through our homes and our loved ones.
Blessed are you now and for ever.

We give you thanks for our own mother
and all she has done for us.
We thank you for her grace and goodness.
We remember all who have cared for us
in our church and society,
all who have shared in our learning and loving.
We ask you to bless the church to which we belong.

Silence

Lord, as we are loved,
help us to love.

We give thanks for all who are newly born into this world.
We ask your blessing upon them,
especially any who will suffer from neglect, violence or abuse.
We remember all unwanted children,
all who are vulnerable or in danger,
all who are born into poverty or famine.
We rejoice in the gift of life and the loving care that is around us.

Silence

Lord, as we are loved,
help us to love.

Lord, thank you for our homes and loved ones.
We thank you today especially for our mother
and all loving relationships.
As we are given tender loving care,
let us show our appreciation by returning that love
in the way we live and in our dealings with each other.

Silence

Lord, as we are loved,
help us to love.

We remember, in your presence,
all who are separated from their loved ones
through illness or circumstance.
We bring before you the needs of the homeless and refugees.
We pray for children who have been taken into care.

Silence

Lord, as we are loved,
help us to love.

God, comfort and strengthen
all who have lost loved ones this year,
especially those who have lost their mother.
We remember all our loved ones departed.
We look forward in faith and in hope to the time
when we can be at home with you in your kingdom.

Silence

Merciful Father,
accept these prayers
for the sake of your Son,
our Saviour Jesus Christ.
Amen.

Fifth Sunday of Lent

YEAR B

Blessed are you, Creator of life and joy.
We give you thanks for the promise of eternal life
offered through the death and resurrection
of your Son, Jesus Christ.
As we rejoice in the gift of this new day
we seek to delight in you and in your great love.
Blessed are you for ever.

We give thanks for all who have helped us
to grow in the faith,
for teachers and preachers, for shining examples,
for friends and relatives.
Bless all who seek to bring others to you,
all who by their goodness
show the world of your goodness.
We remember all who work in mission and outreach.

Silence

Holy and strong God,
help us to reveal your glory.

We give thanks for explorers and inventors,
for all who extend our experience
of the world and its mysteries.
We remember especially all who are involved in research.
We ask you to bless all who work in farming and agriculture,
all who seek to provide us with food.
Help us to care for the hungry and the homeless.

Silence

Holy and strong God,
help us to reveal your glory.

We give thanks for those
who regularly sacrifice their time and energies for us.
We remember especially our parents
and all who care for us.
Lord, as we are loved, help us to show love to others.
We ask your blessing on all who feel unwanted or lonely.

Silence

Holy and strong God,
help us to reveal your glory.

We give you thanks for all medical research,
for the caring of doctors and nurses.
We pray for all who work in the emergency services
and those who risk their lives for others.
Lord, bless all who are ill, in pain or in danger
with an awareness of your love and care.

Silence

Holy and strong God,
help us to reveal your glory.

Glory be to you, O God,
for through our Saviour Jesus Christ
you have opened to us the way to eternal life.
We rejoice in the fellowship of all your saints.
We remember before you
our loved ones who are departed from us.

Silence

Merciful Father,
accept these prayers
for the sake of your Son,
our Saviour Jesus Christ.
Amen.

Palm Sunday

YEAR B

Blessed are you, Lord God of all creation.
You have created us out of your love and for your love.
Help us to welcome you with songs of 'Hosanna',
knowing that you are our strength and our shield.
Help us to welcome Christ our Lord into our lives
as our Lord and Saviour.

Silence

I will give thanks to you, for you answered me,
and have become my salvation.

Lord, by you we are wonderfully created.
Help us to use our talents and lives
to the benefit of others and to your glory.
May your Church be an instrument of peace in the world.
Lord, forgive the divisions of your Church
and help us to see we are one in you.
Help us to work together to bring in your kingdom.

Silence

I will give thanks to you, for you answered me,
and have become my salvation.

Lord, we long for the time
when the kingdoms of the world
may become the kingdom of God.
Help us to work for peace and justice.
Bless the work of all who strive
to maintain and increase peace.
We pray especially for the United Nations.

Silence

I will give thanks to you, for you answered me,
and have become my salvation.

Lord, come and rule in our lives,
that there may be peace in our hearts and in our homes.
We remember before you
homes where there is conflict and violence,
where there is division and distress.

Silence

I will give thanks to you, for you answered me,
and have become my salvation.

God, we bring before you
the troubles and distress of peoples and nations.
We remember the hungry and homeless.
We ask you to bless
all who are not at peace with themselves,
all who are disturbed in mind or spirit.
We ask that all who are ill at this time
may know your love and your presence.

Silence

I will give thanks to you, for you answered me,
and have become my salvation.

We rejoice in the fellowship of all your saints.
We commend ourselves, our loved ones
and the faithful departed
to your love and your saving power.

Silence

Merciful Father,
accept these prayers
for the sake of your Son,
our Saviour Jesus Christ.
Amen.

Easter Day

YEAR B

Blessed are you, God and Father of us all,
giver of life and life eternal.
By the love of your Son you have triumphed over hatred.
In his power, light has conquered darkness
and life has overcome death.
You have opened for us the gate of eternal life.
Blessed are you, O God, now and for ever.

Silence

Lord, we are Easter people:
let 'Alleluia' be our song.

We give you thanks and praise
for the resurrection of our Lord Jesus Christ
and for his appearances to his loved ones.
We rejoice with the whole Church in the joy of the risen Lord.
May we who know the Good News
go and tell others that he is risen.
Grant that your Church may help to bring peace and hope
to a troubled world.
We ask you to give courage to all who have not seen
and yet believe.

Silence

Lord, we are Easter people:
let 'Alleluia' be our song.

Risen Lord, we seek your peace:
peace for our war-torn world;
peace between nations and people;
peace in our dealings with each other;
peace in our hearts and homes.

Silence

Lord, we are Easter people:
let 'Alleluia' be our song.

As you appeared to the disciples in the house,
come enter our homes;
come enter into our fear and darkness;
come enter into our enclosed lives and our fear to venture.
Come with the glorious freedom you offer
to the children of God.

Silence

Lord, we are Easter people:
let 'Alleluia' be our song.

We come with all who weep by gravesides,
all who mourn the loss of a loved one,
all who feel lonely or deserted.
May all who mourn find new hope and joy in you.
We remember all who are terminally ill
and those who are caring for them.
We think of those who have a heavy weight
on their hearts and minds
and tears in their eyes.
We ask that we may all know the hope of eternal life.

Silence

Lord, we are Easter people:
let 'Alleluia' be our song.

We rejoice with the disciples and all your saints
in the joy of the risen Lord.
We ask you to bless all our loved ones departed
with the fullness of your light and peace in eternal life.

Silence

Merciful Father,
accept these prayers
for the sake of your Son,
our Saviour Jesus Christ.
Amen.

Second Sunday of Easter

YEAR B

Blessed are you, Lord God of our salvation.
To you be praise and glory for ever.
You have delivered us from the darkness of death
through your beloved Son.
In him, light has conquered darkness;
life has triumphed over death.
He has breathed into us your life-giving Spirit.
Blessed are you, Father, Son and Holy Spirit,
our God for ever and ever.

Lord, we give you thanks for the light of the Gospel
and that it shines in our hearts.
We rejoice in the resurrection and in your saving power.
We remember all who are struggling with their faith,
those who doubt,
any who sit in darkness or who live in fear.
We bring to mind all who have fallen away from the faith,
especially any known to us.

Silence

Lord God, you are light:
in you is no darkness at all.

We remember peoples and nations who feel drained
and lack energy.
We ask your blessing upon all who suffer
from poverty or oppression.
We pray for any who are separated
from their loved ones and their homes;
we remember all who are in prison.

Silence

Lord God, you are light:
in you is no darkness at all.

We give thanks
that you appeared in an ordinary home, O Christ.
We ask that your presence and your peace
may be known in our homes and among our loved ones.
We bring before you homes
where faith is mocked or persecuted,
and pray for all who are struggling to remain faithful.

Silence

Lord God, you are light:
in you is no darkness at all.

We think of all who are struggling with life:
homes where there is tension or lack of peace;
people who are ill and afraid of the future;
all who are lonely and facing a time of crisis.
May all know your presence and your peace.

Silence

Lord God, you are light:
in you is no darkness at all.

Father, we give you thanks
for the new life that you offer to us in your Son,
for you offer us eternal life.
We come to you with confidence
and pray for friends and loved ones departed.
May they know the fullness of joy in your presence
and in eternal life.

Silence

Merciful Father,
accept these prayers
for the sake of your Son,
our Saviour Jesus Christ.
Amen.

Third Sunday of Easter

YEAR B

Blessed are you, mighty God,
creator of light and darkness.
To you be praise and glory for ever.
By the resurrection of your Son to eternal life
you have destroyed the darkness and fear of death.
Radiant life is ours through him who loves us,
Jesus, our Lord and our Friend.
Blessed are you, Father, Son and Holy Spirit,
our God for ever and ever.

We give thanks that you have called us
to witness to your resurrection and to your presence.
Help us, Lord Jesus, to turn away from sin and to follow you.
May your Church reveal your glory to the world.
We remember today all who are persecuted for their faith,
all who are struggling to make your name known
in difficult areas.
We pray for all who are full of doubt or fear.

Silence

You set us free when we are hard-pressed.
Have mercy on us and hear our prayer.

We bring before you the fearful and the anxious;
all whose lives are in danger through violence or war.
We remember all who are locked away,
in prison or by painful memories,
all who are striving for new freedom and for hope.

Silence

You set us free when we are hard-pressed.
Have mercy on us and hear our prayer.

We give thanks for your presence in our homes:
that you are always with us.
May we know you as a friend and helper.
Bless our family and our loved ones
with your abiding presence.
Be known among our friends and our companions.
We remember all who live alone
and are worried about their lives or their future.

Silence

You set us free when we are hard-pressed.
Have mercy on us and hear our prayer.

We give thanks for the healing power of faith.
We ask you to bless and guide all who heal.
We remember our own doctor and surgery.
We ask that the ill and the weary may know you
as their companion and helper.
We pray to you for all who are hard-pressed
and struggling at this time,
especially for . . .

Silence

You set us free when we are hard-pressed.
Have mercy on us and hear our prayer.

Blessed are you, Lord Jesus Christ,
for you have triumphed over darkness and death,
opening for us the way to eternal life.
We remember in your presence
friends and loved ones who are departed from us.
May they rejoice in the fullness of life eternal.

Silence

Merciful Father,
accept these prayers
for the sake of your Son,
our Saviour Jesus Christ.
Amen.

Fourth Sunday of Easter

YEAR B

Blessed are you, Lord our God.
When we were lost in our sin
you sent our Lord as the Good Shepherd to bring us home.
He descended into the depths to raise us to the heights;
he tasted death for us to know eternal life.
Blessed are you, Father, Son and Holy Spirit.

We give thanks for all who are called
to be shepherds of your people,
all who are guides and protectors.
We remember bishops and especially our bishop;
we pray for all priests and especially our own pastor.
Bless all who teach us the faith
and help us to walk in the way of holiness.

Silence

The Lord is my shepherd;
I shall fear no evil.

We ask you to give courage and strength
to all who work in the emergency services.
We pray for all ambulance crews and paramedics,
for air and sea rescue services
and for coastguards.
We remember the police and the fire crews.
Bless, O Lord, all who work
for the relief of poverty and suffering
among the poor of our world.

Silence

The Lord is my shepherd;
I shall fear no evil.

We give you thanks
for the safety and comfort of our homes.
We ask you to protect our loved ones
and guide them in the ways of peace.
Give wisdom and love to all who work
in the social services.
Comfort all who are lonely or feel unwanted.

Silence

The Lord is my shepherd;
I shall fear no evil.

God of love, we remember all
who have been involved in accidents this week.
We pray for all who have been injured
and those who are bereaved.
We pray for those who have gone into hospital
and all who are ill at home.

Silence

The Lord is my shepherd;
I shall fear no evil.

Good and gracious God,
you have rescued us from the darkness of death
and opened for us the way to eternal life.
We bring before you all our friends and loved ones
who are now with you in your kingdom.
Lord, grant them your love and light.

Silence

Merciful Father,
accept these prayers
for the sake of your Son,
our Saviour Jesus Christ.
Amen.

Fifth Sunday of Easter

YEAR B

Blessed are you, Lord our God,
for you have created us out of your love
and for your love.
We know that we abide in you
and that you are in us
by the Spirit that you have given us.
As you love us, help us to love one another,
Father, Son and Holy Spirit.

Lord, bless the Church with the knowledge
of your indwelling presence.
May we learn to abide in you
and know that you are in us.
Give wisdom to all who go out in mission
and all who preach your word.
We pray for the young in the faith,
that they will be given the opportunity
to grow and bear fruit.
We remember all study groups, Bible classes
and Sunday schools.

Silence

Lord, you abide in us;
we ask that we may abide in you.

We remember the nations of the world
and especially those who are not at peace at this time.
We ask your guidance on all who care
for the world's poor, refugees and war-torn peoples.
We pray for the time when the kingdoms of this world
may become the kingdom of Christ our Lord.

Silence

Lord, you abide in us;
we ask that we may abide in you.

We give thanks for all who have shared their faith with us.
In our turn may we also bear fruit
and bring others to the love and presence of our God.
Lord, bless our homes with the glory of your presence.
Help us to live in and share your peace.

Silence

Lord, you abide in us;
we ask that we may abide in you.

We bring before you all who doubt or despair,
all who are surrounded by darkness or illness.
May they come into the light of your love
and know that you are with them.
We ask you to bless all who have been involved
in accidents or in violence this week.
Give courage and hope to all
who seek to bring your healing and peace.

Silence

Lord, you abide in us;
we ask that we may abide in you.

Lord, you abide with us through life
and we abide with you through death.
In your love you have given us eternal life
through Christ our risen Lord.
We give you thanks for this great gift.
We ask that you bless all our loved ones departed
with the joy of your love and your presence.

Silence

Merciful Father,
accept these prayers
for the sake of your Son,
our Saviour Jesus Christ.
Amen.

Sixth Sunday of Easter

YEAR B

Blessed are you, Lord God, who through your Son
has revealed your great love for us
and in his resurrection gave us a Friend and a Saviour.
We rejoice in your presence this day
with the joy and the freedom of the children of God.
Blessed are you, our God for ever.

As you have called us to be friends,
to reveal your love and the joy of your presence,
we come with sorrow for the divisions
of the Church and the world.
We seek forgiveness for rivalry and disunity within the Church.
Lord, strengthen us in love
and lead us to a unity that reflects that we are one in you.
May any divisions within our community be healed
and well-being restored.

Silence

Lord, as you love us,
help us to love one another.

We come before you as part of a world
caught up in violence, war, hatred, greed and hunger.
There are people who are oppressed and treated as slaves.
There are people who are counted as nothing,
rejected and unloved.
Lord, forgive us and change us.
Strengthen all who work for the peace and well-being of all.
May we share in the care of all suffering people.

Silence

Lord, as you love us,
help us to love one another.

We give you thanks for all our loved ones,
for their generosity and sacrifice for us.
We remember all who feel unloved and unwanted.
We pray for homes where there is hatred or violence,
where there is little respect for each other,
where there is neglect.
We ask your blessing upon all who have been taken into care.

Silence

Lord, as you love us,
help us to love one another.

Lord of love, we remember before you all who are lonely.
We ask your blessing upon those who are ill or injured.
We pray for all who are raging against life
and all who are not at peace with themselves or the world.
We pray for all who have hardened their hearts against love.

Silence

Lord, as you love us,
help us to love one another.

We rejoice in your saving love
and that you have called us to eternal life.
We remember loved ones departed from us.
As we give thanks for their friendship
we pray that they may know you as their friend
in your eternal kingdom.

Silence

Merciful Father,
accept these prayers
for the sake of your Son,
our Saviour Jesus Christ.
Amen.

Ascension Day

YEAR B

Blessed are you, Lord our God.
You have revealed your hidden glory to us
in the face of our Lord Jesus Christ.
Blessed are you, Father, Son and Holy Spirit.

As the church rejoices in the Ascension
we lift our hearts to you, O Lord, on high.
We remember before you
all who are being challenged in their faith,
those who have been brought low by oppression,
persecution or mockery.
We ask your blessing on churches that are struggling to survive,
those that are failing to grow
and those that have lost sight of their mission and outreach.
We seek to share with those who proclaim your love
and your presence.

Silence

We lift up our hearts.
We lift them to you, O Lord.

As we are uplifted by the joy of the Ascension
we remember all who suffer from poverty, violence or war.
We ask your blessing upon all who have lost hope or vision,
all who fear for their future.
We remember those who are forced out of their homes
or off their land.
We pray that the world may move towards a greater freedom and
justice for all peoples.

Silence

We lift up our hearts.
We lift them to you, O Lord.

We give thanks for your great love towards us, O God.
We remember before you our loved ones
and all who are dear to us.
We pray for all who are having difficulties in their relationships.
We remember those who are suffering
from broken relationships, broken homes or broken hearts.
May all know your everlasting love and your abiding presence.

Silence

We lift up our hearts.
We lift them to you, O Lord.

We give thanks for your promise to be with us always
and we remember all who feel lonely or unwanted.
We ask your blessing upon all who suffer
from autism or depression,
all who are caught up in despair
or feel that they are taken for granted.
We remember before you all who are ill at home or in hospital,
all who await a doctor's diagnosis
or who need constant care and treatment.
We ask your blessing on all who work
in the healing professions.

Silence

We lift up our hearts.
We lift them to you, O Lord.

As we rejoice in the glory of your kingdom
and the gift of eternal life
we give thanks for all your saints.
We thank you for all who have revealed your love
and your presence to us.
We pray for our friends and loved ones departed,
that they may rejoice in the fullness of your kingdom.

Silence

Merciful Father,
accept these prayers
for the sake of your Son,
our Saviour Jesus Christ.
Amen.

Seventh Sunday of Easter

YEAR B

Blessed are you, Lord our God.
You are always with us
and ready to hear our prayers.
You have called us by our name
and wait for us to turn to you.
You have chosen us to work with you
and you seek to fill us with your Spirit.
Blessed are you, Father, Son and Holy Spirit.

We give you thanks for men and women of prayer
who have revealed your love
and helped us to know of your presence.
We remember before you
all who are evangelists and ministers,
all who proclaim your love for us.
May we share in the ministry and the outreach
of your Church.

Silence

Lord, as we wait upon you,
hear our prayer.

We bring before you the troubles and the sadness
of our world.
We pray for all who have lost their vision,
who are blind to goodness
and unaware of your presence or your love.
We remember especially
all who feel that life is without purpose and meaningless.

Silence

Lord, as we wait upon you,
hear our prayer.

We thank you for all who love us,
for our families and our friends.
We know that you reveal your love through their love.
We ask your blessing on homes where there is little love
or where there is violence and neglect.
May we welcome you into our homes
and into our friendships.

Silence

Lord, as we wait upon you,
hear our prayer.

We give thanks to all who have been called
to share in your healing powers.
Bless all doctors and nurses,
all who work in hospitals or are part of ambulance crews.
We remember before you all who are struggling with life,
those who are ill or lonely, anxious or depressed.

Silence

Lord, as we wait upon you,
hear our prayer.

We rejoice that our Lord shares in our prayers
and makes intercession for us in heaven.
We pray for all our loved ones who have died
and are now in your keeping.

Silence

Merciful Father,
accept these prayers
for the sake of your Son,
our Saviour Jesus Christ.
Amen.

Pentecost

YEAR B

Blessed are you, Lord our God.
Your Spirit comes to our weakness with his power.
In the strength of your Spirit
you enable us to live and work
to your praise and glory.
May we who have received the gifts of the Spirit
use them for the benefit of your creation
and to reveal your love in the world.
Blessed are you, Lord God,
Father, Son and Holy Spirit.

Lord, as we rejoice in the coming of the Spirit
we give thanks for all who proclaim
your presence and power.
We remember all preachers and evangelists,
all who celebrate the sacraments and minister to us.
May all your people share fully
in forwarding the Gospel and revealing your love.

Silence

We rejoice that you fill our world.
Your Spirit is with us.

Lord, you give great gifts and talents to your people.
We ask you to bless and guide all leaders
of nations and peoples,
all who make decisions that will affect our lives
and the future of the world.
We pray for scientists and research workers,
for all who work in providing us with news
or influence us through the press and television.

Silence

We rejoice that you fill our world.
Your Spirit is with us.

We give thanks that your Holy Spirit
came upon the disciples in an ordinary home.
Bless our homes with your presence
and grant that there we may grow in the fruits of the Spirit.
Let us know you are with our loved ones and us.
Protect us from all evil
and guide us by your Spirit
in the ways of peace and love.

Silence

We rejoice that you fill our world.
Your Spirit is with us.

Lord of life, we remember all who are dis-spirited,
the distressed, the depressed and despairing,
all who have lost hope or joy in their lives.
We pray for all who fear the future,
all who have lost sight of you and your love.
We remember also all who are struggling
with poverty or hunger,
the homeless and the refugee.
We pray for all who are ill.

Silence

We rejoice that you fill our world.
Your Spirit is with us.

We give you praise, Lord, giver of life and life eternal.
We rejoice that you renew, refresh and restore us.
We remember in your presence
your blessed saints and our loved ones departed;
may light perpetual shine upon them
as they share in the glory of your kingdom.

Silence

Merciful Father,
accept these prayers
for the sake of your Son,
our Saviour Jesus Christ.
Amen.

Trinity Sunday

YEAR B

Blessed are you, Lord God, Father of all creation.
To you be praise and glory for ever.
Your Son Jesus Christ brings light
to dispel our darkness and hope to banish our fears.
He sends upon us your promised Spirit
to strengthen and guide us.
Through your great grace and goodness
help us to reveal your love in all the world.
Blessed are you, Father, Son and Holy Spirit.

Father, we give thanks
for the wonders and mystery of creation.
We thank you for life and for your love.
We ask you to bless the nations of the world
as they strive for unity and peace.
We remember all who work in caring for our planet,
all who work in conservation and in growing our food.

Silence

Holy, holy, holy God,
hear us and help us.

Jesus, you are our Redeemer.
You gave yourself in love for us.
We come to give our love to you.
We remember in your presence
all who lack any knowledge of love.
We pray for all who are scorned and rejected,
especially those who suffer
from the cruelty and wickedness of others.
We ask you to bless all who are struggling at this time.

Silence

Holy, holy, holy God,
hear us and help us.

Holy Spirit, inspirer and giver of talents,
we thank you for artists and craftspeople,
for all who beautify and enrich our earth.
We remember in your presence
all who are unable to use their talents
because of the situation in which they live.
We remember those who are restricted
by poverty or tyranny.

Silence

Holy, holy, holy God,
hear us and help us.

Holy and blessed Trinity, Three Persons and One God,
we thank you for your love which is eternal.
We thank you for the gift of personality.
We remember in your presence
friends and loved ones who are departed from us.
May they rejoice in the fullness of life eternal
in your presence and in your kingdom.

Silence

Merciful Father,
accept these prayers
for the sake of your Son,
our Saviour Jesus Christ.
Amen.

Proper 4

Sunday between 29 May and 4 June inclusive
(if after Trinity Sunday)

YEAR B

Blessed are you, Lord our God,
for you have created light to dispel the darkness
and have shone in our hearts
to give the light of the knowledge of the glory of God
in the face of Jesus Christ.
We rejoice that all power and might come from you.
Blessed be God for ever.

Loving God, we pray for all who do not know or love you.
We remember especially
those who have hardened their hearts against you.
We pray for all whose life is joyless
or governed by rules rather than love.
May your Church be willing to accept and welcome
all who come seeking you and your love.
Teach us to be generous in our dealings with each other.

Silence

Lord, bringing light out of darkness,
let us share in your love.

We give thanks for the many talents and abilities of your people.
We rejoice in each other's gifts and uniqueness.
We pray for all who are restricted
by tyranny or the dominance of others.
We remember all who are in refugee camps or are homeless.
We pray for all who feel unloved and neglected.

Silence

Lord, bringing light out of darkness,
let us share in your love.

We thank you for our homes
and the love and acceptance that is there.
We pray for homes where life is oppressive
or adventure smothered.
We remember all who are leaving home for the first time
and all their loved ones.
We give you thanks for homes
where there are new members of the family
and where all are growing in love.

Silence

Lord, bringing light out of darkness,
let us share in your love.

Loving God, we pray for all who walk in darkness
and live in fear.
We think especially of those who are persecuted,
abused or neglected.
We remember before you all who are depressed and lonely,
all who are struggling to survive.
We remember also all who are ill
and all who have been injured in accidents or acts of violence.
We think especially of those who are now disabled
or restricted by illness.

Silence

Lord, bringing light out of darkness,
let us share in your love.

Lord of life, we rejoice
that you have destroyed the darkness of death
and opened for us the way to eternal life.
In love we bring before you our dear ones departed,
praying they may rejoice in your light.
In fellowship with all the saints,
we offer you our love and ourselves.

Silence

Merciful Father,
accept these prayers
for the sake of your Son,
our Saviour Jesus Christ.
Amen.

Proper 5

Sunday between 5 and 11 June inclusive
(if after Trinity Sunday)

YEAR B

Blessed are you, Father, Son and Holy Spirit,
for you reveal your love to us through our families and friends.
We learn of your care and protection
through the goodness and grace of our loved ones.
Teach us to learn to love as you love us.
Blessed are you, Father, Son and Holy Spirit.

We rejoice in the family of the Church.
May all who come find love and fellowship.
May they find acceptance and friendship.
Lord, help your Church be an instrument
of peace and healing in the world.
As we come together,
let us show the unity that is ours in Christ Jesus;
let us show one faith, one Church, one God.
We pray especially for unity among Christians,
that they may show a unity to the world.

Silence

Father, in your mercy,
hear your children's prayer.

We praise you, O God,
for the wonderful variety of people and talents in the world.
We ask your blessing
on all areas of growth in goodness and grace.
We pray for schools, colleges and universities.
Lord, guide all who influence the minds of young people;
we pray for those who work with television
and in the pop-culture of today.

Silence

Father, in your mercy,
hear your children's prayer.

We give thanks for all that enriches and encourages family life.
We pray for the social services
and all who support any families that are in difficulty.
We remember before you families
where there is great debt or where love is absent.
Lord, bless our homes with your love and care.

Silence

Father, in your mercy,
hear your children's prayer.

We give thanks that you are a God who heals and restores,
that you care for our whole being – body, mind and spirit.
We remember in your presence
all who have been injured in accidents or through acts of violence,
all who have taken ill suddenly
and those whose illness has no cure.
We pray for their well-being and the knowledge of your love.
Lord, bless all who share in healing.
We pray for our doctors and nurses
and all who work in hospitals.

Silence

Father, in your mercy,
hear your children's prayer.

Lord, in your power
all are restored and renewed in your heavenly kingdom.
We give thanks for all the saints
and we pray to you for our loved ones and friends
who are departed from us.

Silence

Merciful Father,
accept these prayers
for the sake of your Son,
our Saviour Jesus Christ.
Amen.

Proper 6

Sunday between 12 and 18 June inclusive
(if after Trinity Sunday)

YEAR B

Blessed are you, Lord God.
You give the increase to our sowing,
to our work and to our plantings.
You are the giver of life and life in abundance.
May we put our faith in your goodness
and, when we have sown, trust the increase to you.
Though our faith is often small, it is in a Mighty God.
Blessed are you, Father, Son and Holy Spirit.

We give thanks for those who taught us the faith,
who sowed the seed of the Gospel in our hearts.
We ask your blessing upon preachers and teachers,
upon ministers of the word and the sacraments.
We remember homes where the word of God is sown
and children are given the chance to grow in the kingdom.
We pray for the Bible Society,
for all who produce and translate the Bible.

Silence

Lord our God,
your kingdom come in us as it is in heaven.

Lord, we long for the time when the kingdoms of the world
will become the kingdom of Christ our Lord.
May the rulers on earth reflect the gentle and loving rule
of your kingdom in heaven.
We pray for all who are striving to do your will
in their places of work and in their homes,
for all who witness to you by their way of life.

Silence

Lord our God,
your kingdom come in us as it is in heaven.

We give thanks for those who love us
and show us through their lives a glimpse of your kingdom.
We ask your blessing upon our homes and our loved ones.
We remember all who suffer from violence or neglect
in their homes,
all who feel uncared for or unwanted.
We pray for the lonely and those who have been taken into care.

Silence

Lord our God,
your kingdom come in us as it is in heaven.

We give thanks for the work of healing in our hospitals
and through the healing professions.
We pray for our own doctor.
We remember areas of the world where there is little care
or where the problems seem to overwhelm
those who seek to help.
We remember peoples caught up in disasters,
in floods, in drought or in war.
We pray for relief agencies and all who contribute to them.

Silence

Lord our God,
your kingdom come in us as it is in heaven.

We give thanks for all the saints,
for those who spread the word of God,
for those who witnessed to your love,
for those who brought the Gospel to this land.
We remember all our loved ones who are departed from us
and pray that they may rejoice in the fullness of your kingdom.

Silence

Merciful Father,
accept these prayers
for the sake of your Son,
our Saviour Jesus Christ.
Amen.

Proper 7

Sunday between 19 and 25 June inclusive (if after Trinity Sunday)

YEAR B

Blessed are you, Lord our God,
for you are ever with us
and your presence brings us close
to your power and your peace.
You are ready to hear our cry
and to help us in our troubles.
We rejoice in your love and in your care.
Blessed are you, God, for ever, Father, Son and Holy Spirit.

Almighty and loving God,
we seek to rest in your presence and in your peace.
The Church is often buffeted
by storms of antagonism and opposition.
We remember before you all Christians
who are struggling to survive in areas
where they face violence or ridicule for their faith.
We pray especially for those whose lives are at risk at this time.
We remember also young Christians
who have to face opposition from their friends and relatives.

Silence

Lord, in the storms of life we call upon you:
grant us your peace.

God our Creator, we rejoice in the well-being that is ours.
We remember in your presence all who are suffering at this time
from storms, from floods, from drought.
We pray for all who are caught up in war,
in violence and acts of wickedness.
We remember all who are suffering from poverty
or who are in great debt.

Silence

Lord, in the storms of life we call upon you:
grant us your peace.

We give you thanks for the love and protection of our homes.
Lord, grant that our loved ones
may know your peace and your presence.
We remember homes where people are not coping well,
where there are struggles in relationships.
We remember especially homes where there are great tensions
between parents and their children.
Bless, O Lord, all whose homes have fallen apart
and all children who have been taken into care.

Silence

Lord, in the storms of life we call upon you:
grant us your peace.

God, you are ever-present.
We ask you to strengthen and support
all who are overwhelmed by the storms of life.
We remember those whose sickness finds no cure.
We pray for loved ones and carers who feel exhausted
and unable to cope any more.
Bless, O Lord, all who have been injured this week
or who have gone into hospital,
and all their loved ones who are anxious for them.

Silence

Lord, in the storms of life we call upon you:
grant us your peace.

Mighty God, when the last great storm overwhelms us
help us to know you are there as the Lord and Giver of life;
to know we are not alone and you will not let us perish.
Bless our loved ones who are departed
from the storms and troubles of this world
with your presence and your peace.

Silence

Merciful Father,
accept these prayers
for the sake of your Son,
our Saviour Jesus Christ.
Amen.

Proper 8

Sunday between 26 June and 2 July inclusive

YEAR B

Blessed are you, O God,
our Lord, King of the Universe, God of our fathers,
our Creator, Redeemer, Sustainer.
From you come life, renewal and refreshment.
In you we find hope, restoration and well-being.
We believe in you, we trust you.
Blessed are you, Father, Son and Holy Spirit.

We give thanks for the Church throughout the world;
for people who are growing in the faith
and being made strong by their beliefs.
We remember all who are struggling with opposition and evil
and all whose lives are in danger.
We remember all who feel oppressed and let down.
We pray for all whose faith is being challenged
and those who have lost contact with you.

Silence

Lord, through contact with you
help us to rise.

Lord, we rejoice in the lives and talents
of the people of our world.
We pray to you for all whose gifts are being wasted
through poor education or through tyranny.
We remember all whose ambitions and livelihood
have been destroyed through war or natural disasters.
We ask your blessing upon all who
are counted as untouchable or are rejected by society.

Silence

Lord, through contact with you
help us to rise.

We give you praise and thanks for all who care for us.
We ask your blessing upon our families and friends,
all whom we love and all who love us.
We remember homes were there is serious illness
and where loved ones are carers.
We pray especially for all who are struggling
to keep their homes together,
all whose physical or financial resources are running out.

Silence

Lord, through contact with you
help us to rise.

We give thanks for all healers,
for doctors and nurses, for social workers and carers.
We remember all who are strengthened
by their faith and trust in you.
We ask you to bless all whose sickness finds no cure.
We pray for the terminally ill and all who are in a hospice
or need permanent care in a home.
We pray for all who feel their life is wasting away.

Silence

Lord, through contact with you
help us to rise.

Lord, you are the giver of life and life eternal.
We rejoice in your presence and in your love.
We give you thanks for the resurrection
and the hope of eternal life.
We remember in your presence
our friends and loved ones who are departed from us.
We rejoice in the fellowship of all your saints.
We commend the whole world and ourselves
to your unfailing love.

Silence

Merciful Father,
accept these prayers
for the sake of your Son,
our Saviour Jesus Christ.
Amen.

Proper 9

Sunday between 3 and 9 July inclusive

YEAR B

Blessed are you, Lord God, giver of life and light.
You give us of your love: you give us of yourself.
Open our ears to your call and our hearts to your love.
Send us out in the power of your Spirit
to proclaim the Good News of your saving love
as revealed in our Saviour Jesus Christ.
Blessed are you, Father, Son and Holy Spirit.

We give thanks that you sent Jesus to live among us.
We pray that we may share in his mission,
that we may pass on the message of the Gospel
and show acts of mercy that reveal God's love.
May your whole Church be moved to share
in the ministry that is theirs.
We remember today all involved in the healing ministry.
We ask you to bless all counsellors, spiritual directors
and all who lead us in our ministry.

Silence

Lord, hear us:
show us your loving kindness.

We remember all who are suffering under totalitarian states,
all who are oppressed
and forced to do what they do not want to do.
We ask your blessing on all who are seeking
to bring liberty and freedom to captive peoples.
Give courage and strength
to all who are working for relief agencies
and generosity to all who are called upon
to support them in their work.

Silence

Lord, hear us:
show us your loving kindness.

We give thanks for our homes and loved ones.
Through our families teach us to be sensitive
to the needs of others;
help us to listen carefully and to respond quickly.
We ask your blessing upon all
who have stopped communicating properly with each other,
that they may again be awakened
to those with whom they live and work.

Silence

Lord, hear us:
show us your loving kindness.

We give thanks that you, O God, care for us,
body, mind and spirit.
We remember in your presence all suffering people.
We pray especially for those who feel no one listens or cares.
We ask you to bless all who are homeless,
all who are deeply in debt.
We pray for all who are drug addicts
and all who cannot cope with life.
We remember all who are ill in our own community.

Silence

Lord, hear us:
show us your loving kindness.

We rejoice in the Good News of eternal life.
We remember in your presence
friends and loved ones who are departed from us.
We share with them in the fellowship of all your saints
and commend them and ourselves to your unfailing love.

Silence

Merciful Father,
accept these prayers
for the sake of your Son,
our Saviour Jesus Christ.
Amen.

Proper 10

Sunday between 10 and 16 July inclusive

YEAR B

Blessed are you, the God and Father of our Lord Jesus Christ,
who has blessed us with every spiritual blessing.
You have destined us for the glorious freedom
of the children of God.
You have given us of your love and of yourself.
May we rejoice in your rule
and in the coming of your kingdom.
Blessed are you, Father, Son and Holy Spirit,
one God for ever and ever.

Father, we give you thanks for John the Baptist
and the way he stood against an evil regime.
We thank you for the gift of your kingdom to us.
We rejoice in our freedom
and the freedom of our Church and country.
We ask that your Church may reflect your love
in the way it cares for the outcast and the needy.
We remember all who are persecuted for their faith
or for making a stand against evil.
We pray especially for Christians who are seeking
to improve corrupt societies and governments.

Silence

Show us your loving kindness, O Lord,
and grant us your salvation.

We give you thanks for the work of the United Nations
and its efforts to bring peace and unity to our world.
We pray for all who are caught up in war and violence.
We remember those who have lost loved ones
and those who do not know where their loved ones are.
We ask your blessing on the work of Amnesty International
and all who risk their lives for the freedom of others.

Silence

Show us your loving kindness, O Lord,
and grant us your salvation.

Father, may our homes reflect the love and unity of your kingdom.
Bless our families and friends with the joy of your presence.
We ask your love to strengthen all who are in homes
where there is oppression and where lives are not valued.

Silence

Show us your loving kindness, O Lord,
and grant us your salvation.

God, we thank you for the freedom you have won for us
in our Saviour Jesus Christ.
We remember before you all who are slaves to sin and vice.
We pray for drug addicts, alcoholics,
those who gamble away their lives.
We remember also those who are imprisoned
by their illness or incapacity
and who long for a fuller and richer life.

Silence

Show us your loving kindness, O Lord,
and grant us your salvation.

Lord, we pray for the time when your kingdom will come
on earth as it is in heaven.
We long for justice and freedom for all peoples.
We join our prayers with our loved ones departed
and all your saints,
praying that we may all know your rule
and enjoy your presence.

Silence

Merciful Father,
accept these prayers
for the sake of your Son,
our Saviour Jesus Christ.
Amen.

Proper 11

Sunday between 17 and 23 July inclusive

YEAR B

Blessed are you, Lord of our salvation:
to you be praise and glory for ever.
When we have erred and strayed, you seek us out:
your love searches for us and desires to bring us home
to the light of your presence.
As we rejoice in your Son as the Good Shepherd,
stir in us the same compassion for others as you have for us,
that we may help to reveal your glory in the world.
Blessed are you, Father, Son and Holy Spirit.

Loving God, we give you thanks that you have called us
to share in showing your compassion to the world.
Bless all who are called to be pastors, priests and ministers;
all who preach the word and administer the sacraments.
Give to your whole Church a sense of mission and outreach,
that it may share in your redemption.
We remember before you all who lead retreats and quiet days
and all who help us to see the value of silent prayer
and waiting upon you.

Silence

Lord, we come before you;
in you is our peace.

We give thanks for all those who care for sheep and cattle;
all who provide us with food and the necessities of life.
We ask your blessing
upon all who have been made homeless or stateless:
we pray for asylum seekers and refugees.
We remember in your presence
all who are suffering from hunger or poverty
and we pray for all who are seeking to care for them.

Silence

Lord, we come before you;
in you is our peace.

Loving Father, we give you thanks for our lives
and all that we have.
We seek your blessing upon our homes and our loved ones.
We pray for members of our community
who are suffering from loneliness, debt
or the inability to cope with what is happening to them.

Silence

Lord, we come before you;
in you is our peace.

You are our hope and strength, O Lord.
We come to you for refreshment and renewal.
When we are weak, may we trust in your strength.
When we are fearful, may we turn to you and your light.
We pray for all who are struggling at this time.
We remember before you the troubled in mind
and the distressed in spirit.
We ask your blessing upon friends and loved ones who are ill.
We pray especially for any
who have been recently taken into care.

Silence

Lord we come before you;
in you is our peace.

We give you thanks and praise
that through your Son we shall not perish
but have everlasting life.
We rejoice in the fellowship of all your saints.
We remember before you all our loved ones departed,
praying that they may know the fullness of your kingdom.

Silence

Merciful Father,
accept these prayers
for the sake of your Son,
our Saviour Jesus Christ.
Amen.

Proper 12

Sunday between 24 and 30 July inclusive

YEAR B

Blessed are you, Lord our God,
in your love and care for your creation.
You do not turn away any who come to you.
You come to meet the seekers
and provide refreshment for all who hunger and thirst.
You care for the broken and the fragmented
and want nothing to be lost.
Blessed are you, Father, Son and Holy Spirit.

We come to you, dear Lord, as seekers;
we are hungry for your love and your care.
We ask you to bless all who are pilgrims and seekers,
all who long for an awareness of your presence and your power.
We remember before you
all who bring healing and refreshment to your people.
We pray for preachers and pastors,
for leaders of prayer groups and retreat conductors
and for all places of pilgrimage.

Silence

Lord, have mercy:
let us know your compassion and care.

We give thanks for our daily bread
and for all who provide us with our food and shelter.
We pray for farmers and fishermen,
and all who prepare food for us to eat.
We remember before you all who are hungry and weary.
We ask you to bless all who suffer
from poverty, from famine or from natural disasters.
We pray especially for the world poor
and those who are deeply in debt.

Silence

Lord, have mercy:
let us know your compassion and care.

We give you thanks for the comfort and security of our homes.
Lord, give your blessing to all our loved ones and friends.
We pray for any who may feel lonely or uncared for
within our community.
We remember all carers, social workers and helpers.

Silence

Lord, have mercy:
let us know your compassion and care.

Lord, we bring before you all whose lives are fragmented;
people who are broken in body, mind or spirit.
We remember all who feel shattered and exhausted,
all who long for your healing touch.
We pray for all who seek hope and peace,
that they may come to you and rest in your presence.

Silence

Lord, have mercy:
let us know your compassion and care.

You are the God who takes our weakness and makes us strong.
We come to you as mortals and you offer us immortality.
In your loving presence,
we remember friends and loved ones departed
and ask that not one is lost
but gathered into the fullness of joy in your kingdom.

Silence

Merciful Father,
accept these prayers
for the sake of your Son,
our Saviour Jesus Christ.
Amen.

Proper 13

Sunday between 31 July and 6 August inclusive

YEAR B

Blessed are you, Father, Son and Holy Spirit.
You have created us out of your love and for your love.
You have made our hearts to long for you
and nothing else will fully satisfy them.
Help us to turn to you in our hunger and thirst,
that in you and your love
we may find refreshment and life.
You, Lord, are the giver of life in all its fullness.
Blessed are you, God, for ever.

We give thanks for all who sustain us in life
with their love and care.
Bless those who seek to bring us to the Bread of Life
and all who seek to help to provide us
with our spiritual needs.
We pray for all who celebrate the sacraments
and for those being prepared to make their first Communion.
We remember in your presence
all who are pilgrims and seekers,
those who long for your love and wish to serve you.
We ask you to guide any who feel they have lost their way
and put too much trust in material things alone.

Silence

Lord, you alone
are our strength and hope.

We give you thanks for all who work to provide us
with food and refreshment.
We remember those who provide us with bread:
the farmers, the millers, the bakers and the shops.
We ask you to guide all who are caught up
in materialism and consumerism.
We remember especially all who have lost sight
of the deeper meaning of life.

We pray for all who are unemployed
and those who suffer from hunger or homelessness,
all who lack the necessary resources for their well-being.

Silence

Lord, you alone
are our strength and hope.

Lord, we give thanks for our homes and for all who care for us.
We pray for our friends and our loved ones.
We remember our community: its schools and its places of work.
May all reflect your glory and your love.
Let us be aware of any who are lonely or feel rejected.

Silence

Lord, you alone
are our strength and hope.

We give thanks for the renewing powers of our bodies
and for all who share in the healing and care of others.
We pray for all who feel their lives are empty or meaningless,
all who feel they have wasted their lives or never fully lived.
We remember also friends and loved ones who are ill.

Silence

Lord, you alone
are our strength and hope.

Lord, we put our trust in you.
We believe that in you is the gift of eternal life.
We pray that through you and your love
we may be brought at the last to the fullness of your kingdom.
We remember in your presence the Blessed Virgin Mary
and all the saints departed.
We ask you to bless all our loved ones whom we see no longer.

Silence

Merciful Father,
accept these prayers
for the sake of your Son,
our Saviour Jesus Christ.
Amen.

Proper 14

Sunday between 7 and 13 August inclusive

YEAR B

Blessed are you, Lord our God,
for you provided for your children.
In the wilderness of this world you give us the bread of life.
Lord, grant, as we journey towards the Promised Land,
that we may put our hope and our trust in you.
Blessed are you, Father, Son and Holy Spirit.

Father, we give you thanks that you have called us
to know you and to love you.
You have drawn us to you with bands of love.
Help us to listen and to obey your word.
We pray for all preachers and pastors,
for ministers of the word and of the sacraments.
We remember before you all who do not know or love you
and we ask your blessing upon all
who reach out in mission and love to them.
We pray for any who have lost faith in themselves or in you.

Silence

Lord our God,
our hope is in you.

Lord God, Creator of heaven and earth,
we pray for the nations of the world.
May they find a unity and a peace in you.
We ask your blessing upon the work of the United Nations
and upon all peacekeeping forces.
We pray for areas of the world where there is strife and division,
where people are unable to trust each other,
where people do not listen to each other.
We remember displaced peoples and refugees.

Silence

Lord our God,
our hope is in you.

We thank you for the love and protection of our homes.
We ask your blessing upon our families and friends.
We remember before you
homes where there is division or distrust,
where families are divided.
We pray for all who have been betrayed or deserted.
We remember also all who are leaving home for the first time.

Silence

Lord our God,
our hope is in you.

We give you thanks for our own well-being
and for all that feeds our bodies, minds and spirits.
We remember all who are struggling
with doubt, depression and despair,
all who are having difficulty in their daily lives.
We pray for all who are ill at home or in hospital,
especially those who have no one to care for them or visit them.

Silence

Lord our God,
our hope is in you.

We rejoice that you sustain us with the Bread of Life.
Through our union with Jesus you offer us life eternal.
As we celebrate our communion with the saints,
we remember our friends and loved ones departed
and ask that they may rejoice in the fullness of eternal life.

Silence

Merciful Father,
accept these prayers
for the sake of your Son,
our Saviour Jesus Christ.
Amen.

Proper 15

Sunday between 14 and 20 August inclusive

YEAR B

Blessed are you, Lord our God,
you give us life and love.
We rejoice in your presence that is ever with us.
We give thanks for the offering of Jesus on the cross
and for the memorial we have this Eucharist.
May we remember that he comes to us
and asks us to offer ourselves to him.
Blessed are you, Father, Son and Holy Spirit.

Father, we thank you for the revealing of your Son
in the breaking of the bread and in the taking of the wine.
We pray for all who celebrate the memorial
of the death and passion of Jesus.
We ask you to bless all who strive
for unity and fellowship within the whole Church.
May we show that we are Christians by our love and our sharing.

Silence

Lord, may we abide in you
and know you are with us.

We give thanks for the fruits of the earth
and for all that you have given us.
As we give thanks for our daily bread
we remember all who are celebrating
growth and increase in their lives.
We pray for those in new work
or preparing to go to new schools.
We ask you to bless all artists and craftspeople,
all who enrich our world with their talents and goodness.
We remember all who provide us with food
and our daily needs.

Silence

Lord, may we abide in you
and know you are with us.

We give you thanks and praise for our homes,
for their peace and protection.
We ask your blessing on all homes
where there is disunity or discord.
We pray for all who are suffering
from a breakdown in relationships.
We pray for homes where there is a new birth
or someone newly admitted into their family.

Silence

Lord, may we abide in you
and know you are with us.

We give thanks that Jesus has shared our grief and sorrows.
As we give thanks for the wine of communion,
we remember all whose lives are being out-poured.
We pray for all who are facing pain or weakness,
all who feel diminished by the trials of life.
We remember those whose energies are failing
and any who are finding it hard to cope with life.

Silence

Lord, may we abide in you
and know you are with us.

We celebrate our Communion with you, O God,
and with the whole Church on earth and in heaven.
We rejoice in the resurrection of our Lord.
We pray for all our loved ones departed from us:
may they, with all the saints,
enjoy the fullness of your presence and your kingdom.

Silence

Merciful Father,
accept these prayers
for the sake of your Son,
our Saviour Jesus Christ.
Amen.

Proper 16

Sunday between 21 and 27 August inclusive

YEAR B

Blessed are you, Lord our God;
in you is life and life eternal.
You love us with an everlasting love.
You give us the freedom to turn to you or turn away from you.
You do not compel us to love you
but invite us to know you and your love.
Help us in our desire to know you
and to be more faithful to you.
Blessed are you, God, for ever.

We give you thanks for all your faithful people.
We rejoice in the fellowship of your saints
and all who have been loyal to you.
We remember before you those who are new to the faith
and all who are seeking to deepen their faith.
We pray for all who are tempted to turn their back on you,
those who are troubled by doubt
and all those who are finding their faith a challenge.

Silence

Holy Lord,
our trust is in you.

We give thanks for the gift of power you have given
to peoples and nations.
May we use all our powers to your glory
and the benefit of others.
We remember all who suffer from the misuse of power,
all who are oppressed, the wrongly imprisoned
and those who suffer from violence.
Lord, grant us peace in our hearts and in the world.

Silence

Holy Lord,
our trust is in you.

We give you thanks for those who brought us
to know you and love you.
We remember our teachers and preachers.
We pray for our friends and our families.
May our relationships all reflect
a good relationship with you.
We remember all who have been betrayed in love.

Silence

Holy Lord,
our trust is in you.

We give thanks for all who have committed themselves
to work for your glory and the benefits of others.
We remember all who feel let down, deserted or lonely.
We pray for the persecuted and the marginalised in society.
We ask your blessing on all who are ill at home or in hospital,
on all who seek healing or deliverance.

Silence

Holy Lord,
our trust is in you.

You, Lord, are the giver of life eternal.
We remember before you the faithful departed.
We ask your blessing upon loved ones and friends
who are at rest with you.
May they rejoice in the fellowship of the saints
and the fullness of life eternal.

Silence

Merciful Father,
accept these prayers
for the sake of your Son,
our Saviour Jesus Christ.
Amen.

Proper 17

Sunday between 28 August and 3 September inclusive

YEAR B

Blessed are you, Lord our God.
You give us life, you give us love, you give us yourself.
We come to give our lives and our love to you.
Cleanse us from all our sin
and make a clean heart within us,
that we may do what you want us to do
and be the people you want us to be.

We give thanks for the examples of the saints
in their battle against evil and in their striving to do good.
We remember before you
all who are struggling with temptation,
all who are pulled by divided loyalties.
We pray for those who go through the rituals
but miss the reality.
We ask your blessing on all who are scorned and rejected
because of their relationship with Christ.

Silence

Make our hearts clean, O God;
renew a right spirit within us.

We give thanks for the work of the Social Services
and all who work for the care of others.
We remember before you
all who are caught up in vice or degradation.
We pray for all addicts,
that they may find help and hope.
Bless all who struggle to keep standards
and make a stand against the evils that are around them.

Silence

Make our hearts clean, O God;
renew a right spirit within us.

We rejoice in our homes and in family life.
We thank you for all who have given their lives
in caring for us and in loving us.
We ask your blessing upon our families and friends.
We remember before you all who are lonely,
all who feel uncared for or unwanted.
We pray for all who suffer from neglect
or a breakdown in relationships.

Silence

Make our hearts clean, O God;
renew a right spirit within us.

As we rejoice in life, we remember all who feel
that life is meaningless and empty.
We ask your blessing on the despairing and despondent.
We pray for all who are treated as unclean
through illness or disability.
We remember all who work to combat disease and infections.

Silence

Make our hearts clean, O God;
renew a right spirit within us.

We rejoice in the fellowship of all your saints.
We remember before you all our loved ones departed,
giving thanks for their life and their care.
We offer our hearts and minds and whole being to you,
good and gracious God.

Silence

Merciful Father,
accept these prayers
for the sake of your Son,
our Saviour Jesus Christ.
Amen.

Proper 18

Sunday between 4 and 10 September inclusive

YEAR B

Blessed are you, Lord our God,
for you have called your people
from every tribe, nation and language.
We rejoice that you care for all peoples
and every single individual
and seek to offer each of them your love.
You have called us all to hear your word
and to proclaim your praises.
Blessed are you, Father, Son and Holy Spirit.

We rejoice that your Church is for all people
in all times and in all places.
No one who comes to you is cast out.
May we seek to make your Church open and welcoming to all.
We ask your blessing upon all who are involved
in the outreach and mission of the church.
We remember especially those who seek
to proclaim your love by word and example.
We pray for all who have not heard of you
and your saving grace.

Silence

God, ever with us,
be our strength and our Saviour.

We give thanks for the peace
that you offer to us and to the nations.
We remember before you areas of conflict and violence,
and people caught up in war.
We pray for all who suffer from racial hatred or prejudice,
all who are outcasts or refugees.
We ask your blessing upon the work of the United Nations
and all peacekeeping forces.

Silence

God, ever with us,
be our strength and our Saviour.

We give thanks for those who brought us
to know you and your love.
We pray for all who have taught us and cared for us.
We ask your blessing upon our families and our friends.
We remember before you all who are lonely
or feel uncared for and unwanted.

Silence

God, ever with us,
be our strength and our Saviour.

We give thanks for the gifts of hearing and speech.
We remember all who suffer from deafness
and those who are unable to speak.
We pray for all who suffer from autism,
all who are withdrawn from normal life
and all who find communication difficult.
We ask your blessing upon all ill and suffering people.
We remember especially
friends and members of our community who are ill.

Silence

God, ever with us,
be our strength and our Saviour.

We rejoice that you have opened for us
the fullness of eternal life and the way to your kingdom.
We remember friends and loved ones who are departed from us.
May they enjoy knowing you in glory
and rest in the peace of your presence.

Silence

Merciful Father,
accept these prayers
for the sake of your Son,
our Saviour Jesus Christ.
Amen.

Proper 19

Sunday between 11 and 17 September inclusive

YEAR B

Blessed are you, Lord our God,
for you have sent your Son to be our Saviour.
In the darkness of this world he comes to be our light.
He has triumphed over pain and death
and opened to us the way to everlasting life.
He has revealed your love
and made us sons and daughters of God.
Blessed are you, Father, Son and Holy Spirit.

We give thanks for your saints
and for all who have stood against evil and temptation.
We remember before you all who at this time
are struggling with their faith,
all who are tempted away by false promises and bright lights.
We pray for those who have learnt the words
but not met the Saviour.
We remember any who go through rituals
that seem empty of your presence.
Bless all who are being prepared for confirmation
and all who are seeking to grow in their relationship with you.

Silence

O Lord, our Strength and our Redeemer,
hear our prayer.

We give thanks for the beauty of this day
and for the wonders of creation.
We remember before you all who are suffering
from war or division within communities.
We pray for those who have lost their way in life
and feel life has no meaning or purpose.
We ask your blessing upon all who strive
to improve our world and to create works of beauty.

Silence

O Lord, our Strength and our Redeemer,
hear our prayer.

We give thanks for the support of our families and friends,
for all the encouragement and help they give us.
We pray for homes where there is little encouragement
or where adventure and the fullness of life
are smothered by false securities.
We remember all who are homeless
and uncertain of their future.

Silence

O Lord, our Strength and our Redeemer,
hear our prayer.

We thank you for your love towards us.
We ask you to bless all who are struggling
with temptation and vice at this time.
We pray especially for any who live
in areas of degradation or evil.
We pray for all who struggle with weakness or illness,
especially those who cannot cope on their own.

Silence

O Lord, our Strength and our Redeemer,
hear our prayer.

We give thanks that through Christ we are offered eternal life.
We remember the saints in glory and our loved ones departed.
May they rejoice in your presence
and the fullness of life in your kingdom.

Silence

Merciful Father,
accept these prayers
for the sake of your Son,
our Saviour Jesus Christ.
Amen.

Proper 20

Sunday between 18 and 24 September inclusive

YEAR B

Blessed are you, Lord our God.
You give us the opportunity to meet you
in the call of the poor and in the cries of the needy.
Give us the courage to serve
and to share in the love that you have for all people.
Teach us to be attentive and open to others
for in meeting them we meet you.
Blessed are you, Father, Son and Holy Spirit.

Father, we give you thanks for all who have cared for us
and brought us to know you and your love.
We ask your blessing on all who serve
as ministers and priests within your church.
May our churches be ready
to serve the needs of our community and the world.
We remember all who give their lives
to relieve the sorrows and suffering of their fellow beings.

Silence

Lord, as we draw near to you,
help us to know you are ever with us.

As we rejoice in your goodness and grace,
we remember all who hunger, all who are homeless,
all refugees and stateless peoples.
We remember ethnic minorities
who are suffering from persecution.
We pray for those who suffer through war and violence.
We ask your blessing on all who are underpaid
and treated as slaves
to provide richer people with cheap goods.
We pray for all Fair Trade organisations.

Silence

Lord, as we draw near to you,
help us to know you are ever with us.

We give thanks to you for the love and care in our homes.
We remember how much we are served
and looked after by our parents.
May we never take them or any who care for us for granted.
May we learn to help as much as we can within our own homes.
We ask you to bless all homes
where there is poverty or great debt.
We remember also homes where some individuals
are ignored or taken for granted.

Silence

Lord, as we draw near to you,
help us to know you are ever with us.

Lord, we pray for areas of poverty and bad housing
throughout our world.
We remember all who do not have the basic needs
of care and attention.
We ask your blessing upon all who are ill
and those who feel lonely or neglected.
We remember especially children separated from their loved ones
and children taken into care.

Silence

Lord, as we draw near to you,
help us to know you are ever with us.

Teach us, good Lord, to serve you as you deserve:
to give and not to count the cost.
Grant that we may learn to be generous and gracious
as are your saints who now rejoice in your kingdom.
We rejoice in the fellowship of all your saints
and ask your blessing
upon our loved ones who are departed from us.

Silence

Merciful Father,
accept these prayers
for the sake of your Son,
our Saviour Jesus Christ.
Amen.

Proper 21

Sunday between 25 September and 1 October inclusive

YEAR B

Blessed are you, Lord our God,
for you welcome us whenever we turn to you:
you are always ready to hear us and to help us.
We rejoice in your presence
and ask that we may show your love
and your saving power in the world.
Blessed are you, Father, Son and Holy Spirit.

We give thanks for your Church throughout the world.
May the Church be an instrument
of peace and reconciliation
between peoples and nations.
Bless the churches within our area:
may we learn to work together in unity
and in witness to your saving power.
We pray for churches that are struggling to survive
and that are in areas of hostility or apathy.

Silence

Lord, our Strength and our Redeemer,
hear our prayer.

Father, we give thanks for the peace that you offer us.
We remember in your presence
all who are living in areas of war and violence.
We pray for those who suffer attacks on their communities,
for those who are victims of ethnic cleansing or genocide.
We ask your blessing upon all communities
whose way of life and livelihood are threatened.

Silence

Lord, our Strength and our Redeemer,
hear our prayer.

Father, we thank you for all our loved ones and friends,
for those who have enriched our lives
through their goodness and example.
We ask you to bless and protect them.
We pray for homes where relationships are breaking down,
especially where there is violence or neglect.
We pray for all who are suffering through losing a loved one.

Silence

Lord, our Strength and our Redeemer,
hear our prayer.

Father, we bring to your love
the suffering and sorrow of our world.
We remember in your presence all who are ill
at home or in hospital.
We pray for those involved in accidents
or acts of cruelty and violence this week.
We bring before you all who live in fear
and those who feel they can no longer cope with life.

Silence

Lord, our Strength and our Redeemer,
hear our prayer.

Father, you created us for yourself and for your love.
As we give our love to you,
we pray for all our loved ones who are departed from us.
May they rejoice in the light of your presence
and in the fullness of eternal life.

Silence

Merciful Father,
accept these prayers
for the sake of your Son,
our Saviour Jesus Christ.
Amen.

Proper 22

Sunday between 2 and 8 October inclusive

YEAR B

Blessed are you, Lord our God,
for you have created the world and all that is in it
out of your love and for your love.
You offer us a relationship with you
through your creation and through each other.
Teach us to care for your world and to respect all peoples.
Blessed are you, Father, Son and Holy Spirit.

We give you thanks and praise for the beauty of the earth
and the wonders of each creature.
Lord, help us to have a reverence and awe
for all that you have made.
May your Church encourage a sense of wonder
in all our dealings.
We remember the Church working among oppressed peoples
and all who are treated as unimportant or dispensable.
Let us all learn good stewardship
of the gifts and the world you have given to us.

Silence

God our Creator,
in your love, hear us.

We praise you for the diversity of life on our planet,
for the balance of nature and the goodness of the earth.
We ask your blessing on areas and creatures that are endangered.
We pray for the people of the rain forests
and for primitive tribes that are being robbed of their land.
Lord, guide the decisions of all who influence
the future of the earth.
We pray for multinational companies
and for all who wield power.

Silence

God our Creator,
in your love, hear us.

We give you thanks for all who have shown us love and care.
We remember before you our families and friends
and all our loved ones.
We ask your blessing on all who feel lonely,
all who are neglected
and all whose relationships are breaking down.
We pray for any who have lost a loved one this week
or who have been deserted by a loved one.

Silence

God our Creator,
in your love, hear us.

As we rejoice in life
we pray for all who are doing genetic research
and all who probe into the mystery of life.
May your blessing be upon all who make discoveries
that deeply influence our lives.
We remember all who are struggling.
We pray for those who have lost any sense of wonder or joy,
the depressed and the disillusioned.
Lord, comfort all who are ill
and all who are finding life difficult.

Silence

God our Creator,
in your love, hear us.

We give thanks for the mystery of our own life
and that you are with us always.
We ask your blessing on all who have departed from us
and pray that they may rejoice
in the glory of your presence in your kingdom.

Silence

Merciful Father,
accept these prayers
for the sake of your Son,
our Saviour Jesus Christ.
Amen.

Proper 23

Sunday between 9 and 15 October inclusive

YEAR B

Blessed are you, Lord God of all creation.
Through your goodness we live in a rich and wonderful world.
You have given us the stewardship of your creation.
Lord, help us to work together
for the benefit of your whole world
and to reveal your glory within it.
May we strive for the protection and care
of all you have given into our charge.
Blessed are you, Father, Son and Holy Spirit.

God our Creator, we give you thanks
for the mystery of life and the beauty of the earth.
We remember in your presence
all who strive to reveal your glory.
We pray for churches throughout the world that seek
to help in the care and protection of the environment.
We ask your blessing on church groups
that work in areas of deprivation
and with people that are counted as of little importance.
We pray for all relief organisations
and those working with the world's poor.

Silence

Lord, in your love and goodness,
hear our prayer.

We give thanks for all who enrich our lives
by their talent and care.
We ask you to bless all who influence our future
by the decisions they make in governments
or in multinational companies.
We pray for the work of all who are involved
in conservation and in Fair Trade.
We remember the unemployed
and all who are denied human rights.
We ask your blessing upon all oppressed and homeless people.

Silence

Lord, in your love and goodness,
hear our prayer.

We give thanks for our homes, our talents
and all that you have given to us.
May we use our resources for the benefit of those in need
and for the improvement of the world around us.
Bless our homes, that they may reflect your love
and be where your peace and your presence
are known to abide.

Silence

Lord, in your love and goodness,
hear our prayer.

Lord God, giver of life and health,
we come in our weakness to your strength,
in our troubles to your peace.
We ask your blessing upon all who are suffering,
all who are ill at home or in hospital.
We give thanks for the talent and attention of doctors,
nurses and all in the caring professions.
We pray especially for all who feel lonely or neglected
and all who have no one to care for them.

Silence

Lord, in your love and goodness,
hear our prayer.

Holy and merciful God, we rejoice in your saving power
and that you give us life that is eternal.
We ask your blessing upon all the saints
who have revealed your glory by their lives.
We remember also all who have enriched us
by their goodness and care,
and we pray for all our loved ones and friends
who are departed from us.

Silence

Merciful Father,
accept these prayers
for the sake of your Son,
our Saviour Jesus Christ.
Amen.

Proper 24

Sunday between 16 and 22 October inclusive

YEAR B

Blessed are you, Lord our God.
You have created us out of your love
and redeemed us by your love.
In the offering of our Lord Jesus on the cross
you have freed us from sin
and opened to us the way to eternal life.
Grant that, as Christ came not to be served but to serve,
we may give our lives in your service
and to the benefit of your world.
Blessed are you, Father, Son and Holy Spirit,
one God now and for ever.

Gracious God, you give us life and love.
Help us to give our life and love to you.
May the Church seek to serve the world and to give itself
for the benefit of the communities in which it lives.
We ask you to bless all who are working
among the poor and the destitute.
We pray for prison visitors
and those who reach out in love
to the outcasts and the neglected.
Bless the work of Christian Aid and all relief organisations.

Silence

Lord, our Saviour and Redeemer,
hear us and save us.

We give thanks for the caring professions
and for all who give their lives in the service of others.
We pray for doctors and nurses.
We remember the social services and care workers.
We ask your blessing upon all children who are in homes
or who are in need of protection.
We pray for the Children's Society
and all who work looking after children.

Silence

Lord, our Saviour and Redeemer,
hear us and save us.

Lord, we thank you for those
who have given us of themselves in love and care.
We pray for our parents and our families.
We ask you to bless all who have enriched us
by their goodness and their sacrifice for us.
Lord, teach us to be generous in our dealings
and sensitive to the needs of others.

Silence

Lord, our Saviour and Redeemer,
hear us and save us.

As we rejoice in your saving power,
we remember before you all who work in the rescue services.
We pray for firefighters and ambulance workers,
for the lifeboat teams and the air and sea rescue crews.
We pray for all who have been involved in accidents this week,
remembering the injured and the bereaved.
We ask your blessing upon all who are ill at home or in hospital.

Silence

Lord, our Saviour and Redeemer,
hear us and save us.

Lord, we give thanks
that through the death and resurrection of Jesus
you have opened for us the way to life eternal.
We pray for all who have served you faithfully here on earth
and are now in the fullness of your kingdom.
We remember our friends, benefactors and loved ones
who are departed from us:
may they be at peace with you.

Silence

Merciful Father,
accept these prayers
for the sake of your Son,
our Saviour Jesus Christ.
Amen.

Proper 25

Sunday between 23 and 29 October inclusive

YEAR B

Blessed are you, Lord our God.
You created light out of darkness
and gave us eyes to see the beauty and wonders of your creation.
Lord, through the visible things of this world
lead us to see the invisible;
extend our vision beyond our eyes
that we may see with our hearts also.
Blessed are you, Father, Son and Holy Spirit.

We give thanks for the beauty and colour of our world,
for the gift of sight.
We ask your blessing upon men and women
who help us to see beyond the obvious,
upon all who are prophets and visionaries.
We pray for all who study your word
and who celebrate your sacraments.
We remember those training for ministry
and ask your blessing upon theological colleges
and all who teach Religious Education.

Silence

Lord, open our eyes
to see the invisible.

We give thanks for explorers, discoverers and inventors;
for all who have enriched the world by their wisdom
or by extending themselves.
We ask your blessing upon the leaders of nations,
upon governments and ruling bodies.
We pray for the United Nations and all peacekeeping forces.
We remember today all writers and broadcasters,
artists and craft workers,
and all who influence our lives by their actions.

Silence

Lord, open our eyes
to see the invisible.

We rejoice in the protection and the peace of our homes.
We thank you for our families and friends
and ask your blessing upon them.
We pray for families who have become bored with life
and with each other,
for couples who have lost the spirit of exploration
and adventure.
We ask your blessing upon all who influence
the minds of the young and the vulnerable.

Silence

Lord, open our eyes
to see the invisible.

Lord we give thanks for all who have guided us
into the ways of goodness and love,
all who have enriched our lives by their wisdom.
We remember before you all who have lost their way in life.
We pray for the confused, the disillusioned and the despairing.
We remember all who are ill at home or in hospital.
We pray especially for all who suffer from blindness
or partial vision.

Silence

Lord, open our eyes
to see the invisible.

Lord, open our eyes to your kingdom that is growing among us;
let us see your presence and love at work.
We give thanks for your saints
and for all our loved ones who have departed this life.
May they rejoice where faith has vanished into sight
in the glory of eternal life.

Silence

Merciful Father,
accept these prayers
for the sake of your Son,
our Saviour Jesus Christ.
Amen.

All Saints' Day

1 November or Sunday between 30 October and 5 November inclusive

YEAR B

Blessed are you, Lord our God,
for you have called us out of darkness
into your own most marvellous light.
Grant that our lives may help to reveal
your love and glory in the world.
As you have called each of us to be saints
may we be worthy of our calling.
Blessed be Father, Son and Holy Spirit.

O Lord God, we rejoice in the fellowship of all your saints.
We thank you for (*N*), our patron saint
and for this church in his/her name.
Bless all who are striving to live godly and holy lives.
We remember in your presence all who are growing in the faith,
those in Sunday schools, study groups and confirmation classes.
We pray for all who feel called to be priests, deacons
or teachers of the faith.

Silence

Lord, make us to be numbered with your saints
in glory everlasting.

We give thanks for all who have served the world
in their vocation.
We pray for kings and queens, princes and rulers.
We remember Elizabeth our queen.
We ask your blessing and guidance on all
who hold positions of authority
or who influence the lives of others.
We pray for all who quietly give themselves
in the service of the community in which they live.

Silence

Lord, make us to be numbered with your saints
in glory everlasting.

As we give thanks for our homes and loved ones,
make us aware of the quiet sacrifice and love
that is often given unheeded.
We thank you for all that our parents have done for us
and for any who have been benefactors in our lives.
We ask your blessing upon all who suffer
from violence or neglect in their homes,
all who are discouraged and disheartened
and any who lack a good example to follow.

Silence

Lord, make us to be numbered with your saints
in glory everlasting.

We give thanks for the saints who have triumphed
through suffering
and have revealed your glory despite persecution and pain.
We ask your blessing upon all who are struggling at this time.
We remember those caught up in vice, drugs or crime
and who cannot find a way out.
We pray for victims of terrorism or war,
remembering stateless and homeless people.
We bring before you friends and loved ones who are ill
and all who fear the future.

Silence

Lord, make us to be numbered with your saints
in glory everlasting.

We give thanks for all who have served you on earth
and now are at rest in your kingdom.
We pray for friends and loved ones who are departed from us,
asking that as they shared their love with us on earth
they may know your love in eternal life.
We rejoice in the fellowship of all your saints
and pray that we may share with them
in your eternal kingdom.

Silence

Merciful Father,
accept these prayers
for the sake of your Son,
our Saviour Jesus Christ.
Amen.

Fourth Sunday before Advent

Sunday between 30 October and 5 November inclusive; for use if the Feast of All Saints was celebrated on 1 November and alternative propers are needed

YEAR B

Blessed are you, Father, Son and Holy Spirit,
the one and only God:
to you be praise and glory for ever.
We love you, O God, with all our heart, with all our soul,
with all our mind and with all our strength.
We come to give ourselves to you as you give yourself to us.
Blessed be God for ever.

Father, we give thanks for all who have loved you deeply
and revealed your love to us.
We pray for all who teach from the Scriptures
and for all who preach.
We remember the young in the faith
and pray for their enthusiasm.
We remember also all who have served you for a long time;
may they still have warm hearts and a living faith.
We ask you to bless all who minister in your name.
May the Church reveal your love
and your glory in the world.
We pray for all who seek to dedicate themselves to you
through baptism, confirmation and ordination.

Silence

God of love and mercy,
hear us as we call to you.

We give thanks for all who have used their minds
to improve and care for our world.
We ask you to guide the work of scientists, inventors
and explorers.
We pray for all who seek to expand our knowledge
and who work on the boundaries of science.
We ask you to give wisdom to all who deal with
genetic engineering in humans and in plants.

We pray for musicians and artists,
for craftspeople and all who enrich our world.

Silence

God of love and mercy,
hear us as we call to you.

We give thanks for our homes
and all places where we have learnt of love.
We ask your blessing upon our families and friends.
We pray for all who feel unloved and unwanted,
for the neglected
and all who suffer from violence or cruelty.

Silence

God of love and mercy,
hear us as we call to you.

We give thanks for our talents and abilities
and we remember before you all whose powers are waning
or who feel that they cannot cope with life.
We pray for all who are weakened by illness or circumstance,
all who are deeply in debt.
We ask your blessing upon those who feel unfulfilled
or thwarted in leading a meaningful and joyful life.

Silence

God of love and mercy,
hear us as we call to you.

We give thanks that you love us with an everlasting love.
When we forget you, you do not forget us.
We rejoice in the promise of life eternal
and remember in your presence
the saints who gave themselves fully to you.
We pray for all our loved ones who are departed from us.

Silence

Merciful Father,
accept these prayers
for the sake of your Son,
our Saviour Jesus Christ.
Amen.

Third Sunday before Advent

YEAR B

Blessed are you, Lord our God,
for you have called us out of darkness
into your most glorious light.
In calling us, you give our lives direction and purpose:
you offer us the opportunity
to reveal your love and your presence to the world.
Blessed are you, Father, Son and Holy Spirit,
one God now and for ever.

Lord, we give thanks that you have called us
to know you and love you; keep our ears open to your call
and our hearts open to your love.
Bless, O Lord, each in their vocation,
that every life may be filled
with purpose and meaning through you.
We pray for all who feel thwarted in their vocations
by circumstance or illness;
may they know that God still calls them where they are.
We pray for the Mission to Seafarers
and all who care for those who work on the sea.

Silence

Lord you have called us:
help us to fulfil our calling.

We give thanks for all who are called
to govern and guide the nations of the world.
We ask your blessing on Elizabeth our queen.
We pray for all who are called
to bring peace and maintain peace throughout the world.
We remember before you all who work upon the sea,
fishermen and merchant seamen,
all who are crewing lifeboats and who are coastguards.

Silence

Lord you have called us:
help us to fulfil our calling.

We give thanks for those who have taught us
of you and your love,
for those who have guided us in awareness of you.
We ask your blessing upon our homes,
our families and friends.
May we reveal your glory in our lives.
We remember all who are called to be parents
and ask your blessing upon them and their children.
We pray for any who feel unable to cope
with their families or with relationships.

Silence

Lord you have called us:
help us to fulfil our calling.

Holy and strong One, we remember before you
all who suffer from weakness or illness,
all who suffer from being handicapped
or restricted in their lives.
May they know that you love them and continue to call them.
We ask your blessing on all who are called to work
in hospitals, surgeries and health centres.
We pray for friends and loved ones who are ill.

Silence

Lord you have called us:
help us to fulfil our calling.

Lord, you call us to yourself and to life eternal.
May we learn to enjoy you and our calling this day and for ever.
We rejoice in the fellowship of all your saints.
We pray for our friends and loved ones
who are departed from us.
May we with them have a share in your eternal kingdom.

Silence

Merciful Father,
accept these prayers
for the sake of your Son,
our Saviour Jesus Christ.
Amen.

Second Sunday before Advent

YEAR B

Blessed are you, Lord our God.
You never leave us or forsake us.
You have promised us the victory
through our Lord Jesus Christ.
Lord, help us to know you and to trust in you always.
Let us know that in you is the gift of life eternal
and that through you we have the power
to survive whatever happens to us or to the world.
Blessed are you, God Almighty, Father, Son and Holy Spirit.

We give thanks for those who have taught us the faith
and brought us to know you, O God.
We ask your blessing on preachers and teachers of the Word,
upon theological colleges and their students.
We remember any who are struggling with their faith at this time,
all who are tempted to despair and to give up.
We pray especially for all who are sorely troubled
by circumstances or relationships.

Silence

Lord, in our darkness,
let your light shine.

As we give thanks for the world and its beauty,
we remember before you all areas of conflict and disaster.
We ask your blessing upon all who are suffering
from natural disasters such as flood or famine,
all who are driven off their land by war or tyranny.
We pray for all who are denied minimum rights and wages
and those who live as slaves.
We ask your blessing on all who work
for the good of the world and humankind.

Silence

Lord, in our darkness,
let your light shine.

We give thanks for our homes and our loved ones.
We pray for all families who are suffering
from a breakdown in relationships,
where there is tension and discord,
where there is violence or neglect.
We ask your blessing upon all who are seeking
to improve the neighbourhood in which they live.
We pray for counsellors and carers.

Silence

Lord, in our darkness,
let your light shine.

We rejoice in your love and care for us at all times.
We remember before you
all who have faced trouble or disaster this week.
We ask your blessing upon those who are ill
and whose illness finds no cure;
on all who have been injured in accidents
or who have suffered at the hands of others.
We pray especially for those whose future looks bleak
and who live in fear.

Silence

Lord, in our darkness,
let your light shine.

We give thanks for your everlasting love.
We rejoice in the saints who have witnessed to you
and to their faith in life eternal.
We remember friends and loved ones
who have departed from us
and pray that they may rejoice in the fullness of your love
and their presence in your kingdom.

Silence

Merciful Father,
accept these prayers
for the sake of your Son,
our Saviour Jesus Christ.
Amen.

Christ the King

YEAR B

Blessed are you, Lord our God, King of the Universe.
All things are in your control and in your power
for you are almighty.
In the troubles and darkness of our world
help us to know your presence and your love.
May we know that though we are beset by many troubles
we cannot for a moment fall out of the everlasting arms
and that we are on our way to everlasting life
in the fullness of your kingdom.
Blessed are you, almighty and ever-loving God,
Father, Son and Holy Spirit.

We rejoice this day that Jesus is the King of kings
and Lord of lords.
We give thanks that through him we have the victory and triumph
over all that would seek to defeat us.
We pray that your Church may walk with confidence,
trusting in you and your love.
May we reveal your loving care for the whole of your creation.
We remember Christians who are struggling
to bring peace and love to areas of hatred and strife.
Lord, may each of us seek to do your will.

Silence

Lord, your kingdom come.
Your will be done.

We look forward to the time when the kingdoms of the world
will become the kingdom of Christ the King.
We remember this day all who are suffering
from tyranny or despotic rulers.
We pray for any who feel that life is beyond their control
and all who feel utterly helpless.
Lord, bless all who strive to bring freedom and prosperity
to the peoples of the world.

Silence

Lord, your kingdom come.
Your will be done.

We give thanks that you are our guide and helper in all of life.
We ask your blessing on our homes and our loved ones.
May your kingdom be revealed and your will be done
in all that we do and say.
We pray for families who are suffering at this time from debt and poverty,
from difficulties in relationships and
from watching a loved one who is ill.

Silence

Lord, your kingdom come.
Your will be done.

We rejoice, O Lord, in your saving power.
We remember before you all who are ill at home or in hospital,
all who struggle to survive and all who are oppressed in any way.
We ask your blessing upon all who will find this a difficult week,
those who will have to face hard decisions
and those who feel they have little or no freedom.

Silence

Lord, your kingdom come.
Your will be done.

We put our trust in you, O God,
and in the promise of the fullness of your kingdom.
We remember before you all who have departed from this world
and are now at peace with you.
We pray for loved ones and friends who have died.
We rejoice in the fellowship of all the saints
and pray that we may share with them in your eternal kingdom.

Silence

Merciful Father,
accept these prayers
for the sake of your Son,
our Saviour Jesus Christ.
Amen.

Year C

First Sunday of Advent

YEAR C

Blessed are you, Lord our God,
for you are an ever-present help in our troubles.
You are our strength, our song and our salvation.
We come before you in faith and seek your love.

We give thanks for the Church throughout the world
and for all who have kept faith in you.
We remember all who are being persecuted for their faith,
all who are being scorned or rejected because of their beliefs.
We ask you to give new courage and hope
to those who have lost faith and all who walk in darkness.

Silence

God, our love and our light,
come to us and lighten our darkness.

We give thanks for the land in which we live
and we ask your blessing upon all who are leaders
in government and in society.
We pray especially today for areas
where law and order seem to have broken down.
We ask your blessing upon any who are suffering
from disasters, flood or famine.

Silence

God, our love and our light,
come to us and lighten our darkness.

We praise you for all the love we have received
and we ask you to protect and guide all our loved ones.
Bless our homes and our families with your gift of love.
We pray especially today for any who are suffering
from the breakdown of family life
or from broken or strained relationships.

Silence

God, our love and our light,
come to us and lighten our darkness.

Lord God, giver of life,
we thank you for our well-being
and we remember before you all who are ill or suffering,
all who are finding life overwhelming
and all who cannot cope.
We pray especially for those who are lonely
and feel no one cares.

Silence

God, our love and our light,
come to us and lighten our darkness.

God, giver of life,
we thank you for life in all its fullness
and we remember in your presence
friends and loved ones who are departed from us.
We pray especially
for all who have lost their lives this week
in acts of violence or in accidents.
May they rejoice in life eternal.

Silence

Merciful Father,
accept these prayers
for the sake of your Son,
our Saviour Jesus Christ.
Amen.

Second Sunday of Advent

YEAR C

Blessed are you, Lord God of Israel,
for you come to your people and set them free.
Through the light of Christ
you deliver us from darkness and the shadow of death
and guide us into the way of peace.

As we remember John the Baptist and all the prophets,
we give thanks for men and women of vision through the ages.
We ask you to guide and bless
all preachers of the word and ministers of the sacraments,
all who teach the faith and all who influence our daily lives.
We pray for all who are struggling for freedom in their faith
and for those who are imprisoned because of their beliefs.

Silence

Lord, open our eyes to your presence
and our hearts to your coming among us.

We give thanks for those who do research,
all scientists and biologists,
for all responsible for our health and well-being.
We ask your blessing upon all doctors and nurses.
We pray for the World Health Organisation
and for all who strive to free us from disease and illness.

Silence

Lord, open our eyes to your presence
and our hearts to your coming among us.

Lord, help us to know your presence in our homes.
We ask you to protect and guide our loved ones
in to the ways of peace.
We remember before you all who suffer
from oppression or violence in their homes.

Silence

Lord, open our eyes to your presence
and our hearts to your coming among us.

We give thanks for your love and healing power
and ask your blessing upon all who are suffering,
all who long for freedom
and all who are caught up in debt.
We pray for any who have lost their homes
or their work at this time,
especially any who have been separated from loved ones.

Silence

Lord, open our eyes to your presence
and our hearts to your coming among us.

We give thanks
that you have delivered us from the darkness of death
and offered us the light of life eternal.
We rejoice in the fellowship of all your saints
and we pray for friends and loved ones
who are departed from us.

Silence

Merciful Father,
accept these prayers
for the sake of your Son,
our Saviour Jesus Christ.
Amen.

Third Sunday of Advent

YEAR C

Lord our God, we give you thanks
and rejoice in the great love that you have for us:
we rejoice in your presence and in your peace.
We pray for your whole Church
as it prepares for the Christmas season.
May it encourage people to come before you
in joy and in celebration.
Bless all who preach and all who teach the faith:
may they show the joy of knowing you and your love.
We pray today for all who are burdened with guilt
or with living only by the law.

Silence

God, ever present,
reveal yourself in peace and joy.

We give thanks for places of relaxation and refreshment.
We pray for all who help us to enjoy life and to live in peace.
We remember in your presence all who are over-worked
or heavily burdened.
We remember all who are deeply in debt
or who feel that they cannot cope with life.
We ask your blessing upon all who are finding life hard
or who are lonely.

Silence

God, ever present,
reveal yourself in peace and joy.

We give thanks for our homes and our loved ones.
Bless our families and our friends
with an awareness of you and your love.
We pray for all who suffer from broken homes
or homes where there is violence or abuse.

Silence

God, ever present,
reveal yourself in peace and joy.

We seek your blessing
upon all who are oppressed or depressed,
upon all whose lives are filled with sorrow or pain.
We remember those who are battling with a long-term illness
and those who feel they are losing mobility or agility.
We remember in your presence
all who are struggling at this time.

Silence

God, ever present,
reveal yourself in peace and joy.

We give thanks for the gift of life and for life eternal.
We pray for loved ones departed
and for all who have entered the joy of your kingdom.

Silence

Merciful Father,
accept these prayers
for the sake of your Son,
our Saviour Jesus Christ.
Amen.

Fourth Sunday of Advent

YEAR C

God, we thank you for the obedience of Mary
and for all who help to bring in your kingdom
by seeking to do your will.
We give thanks for your faithful people throughout all ages.
Lord, guide your Church
that it may know your will and serve you faithfully.
We pray for the Church working in areas of poverty,
war or oppression.
May we all strive to reveal your love and your peace.
We ask your blessing on this congregation
as we seek to serve you.

Silence

Lord, guide us:
let your kingdom come among us.

We pray for the time when the kingdoms of this world
will become the kingdom of God.
We look forward to when there will be peace
upon the whole earth.
We pray for the work of all peacemakers,
for the United Nations and all peacekeeping forces.
We ask your blessing upon all who are caught up
in war or terrorism at this time.

Silence

Lord, guide us:
let your kingdom come among us.

We give thanks for the Blessed Virgin Mary,
for welcoming Jesus into her life.
May we know your presence in our homes
and seek to bring in your kingdom through our actions.
We pray for all families who are going through difficult times
and who are struggling.

Silence

Lord, guide us:
let your kingdom come among us.

We give thanks for all who care for the ill and the suffering.
We ask your blessing
upon the work of doctors and nurses,
upon hospitals and hospices.
We remember all who are ill
or who have been injured in accidents
or through acts of violence.
We pray for them and their loved ones.

Silence

Lord, guide us:
let your kingdom come among us.

We pray for all our loved ones departed from us,
who are now in the fullness of your kingdom.
We rejoice in the fellowship of all your saints,
giving special thanks today for the Blessed Virgin Mary.

Silence

Merciful Father,
accept these prayers
for the sake of your Son,
our Saviour Jesus Christ.
Amen.

Christmas Day

YEAR C

Glory be to God in the highest,
to our God who has come among us
and taken upon him our flesh.
God, we give you thanks and praise
for your wonderful gift of yourself.
Help us to know your presence in our lives and in our homes.

We rejoice with the whole Church
as it celebrates your love for us.
We ask your blessing upon any churches
where there is oppression or persecution at this time.
We pray for all who will preach the word
and celebrate the sacraments
today and throughout this season.
We pray for those who will celebrate
in refugee camps and prisons
or completely on their own.
We remember those who would have liked
to have been with us in our worship.

Silence

Jesus, proclaimed by the angels, born of Mary,
come and abide with us.

We give thanks for the message of the angels
and we pray for peace on earth
and goodwill among all peoples.
We pray for all who are caught up in war or violence at this time.
We remember the world's poor, the homeless
and any who live in fear or anxiety.
We pray for all who feel neglected or unwanted.

Silence

Jesus, proclaimed by the angels, born of Mary,
come and abide with us.

We give thanks that our Lord was born into an ordinary family
and lived in an ordinary home.
We ask your blessing
upon all our loved ones and friends this Christmas:
may we know your presence in our joys and celebrations.
We remember all who have to spend this Christmas
away from their homes and loved ones.

Silence

Jesus, proclaimed by the angels, born of Mary,
come and abide with us.

We give thanks that Christ became human
that we might share in the Divine;
that through Christ is our salvation.
We pray for all who are ill or unable to enjoy life.
We remember those who are fearful for their future
or who are unable to cope with the present.
Lord, may they know your love and care for them.

Silence

Jesus, proclaimed by the angels, born of Mary,
come and abide with us.

We give thanks that you came to earth to lift us into heaven.
You took upon you our life
that life could be eternal.
We remember loved ones who have died this year
and those with whom we have spent Christmases past.
Lord, grant to them the gift of life and joy eternal.

Silence

Merciful Father,
accept these prayers
for the sake of your Son,
our Saviour Jesus Christ.
Amen.

First Sunday of Christmas

YEAR C

Blessed are you, Lord our God,
for in your great love for us
you sent your Son into the world.
Blessed are you, Lord Jesus Christ,
for you are one with us
and through you we have life eternal.
Blessed are you, Holy Spirit of God,
for you come to us and inspire us.

We give thanks for the early days of Jesus at Nazareth,
for his learning and his growing.
We pray that the Church may be ready
to nurture young people in their faith,
so that they may grow in spirit as well as in mind and body.
We ask your blessing upon Sunday schools,
Bible classes, Confirmation classes
and all places of learning within the Church.
Guide with your Holy Spirit
all who are called to teach the faith and all who preach the word.

Silence

Lord, ever present,
help us to rejoice in your love and power.

We give thanks for our knowledge and experience
and ask your blessing upon all who have taught us.
We pray for schools, colleges and universities.
We ask your blessing on all who learn through their work.
Lord God, guide all who influence our minds and spirits
through the media, through television and CDs,
through music and through films.

Silence

Lord, ever present,
help us to rejoice in your love and power.

We give thanks for the care and protection of our homes,
especially for all who have shared their lives
and their love with us.
We pray for all who come from homes
where there is discouragement
or a lack of love and understanding.
We remember especially
any children who have been taken into care.

Silence

Lord, ever present,
help us to rejoice in your love and power.

We give thanks for the wisdom of doctors and nurses
in their care for all who are ill.
We pray for all who are suffering at this time,
especially any who have been separated from a loved one
or who have lost a child.
We pray for children separated from loved ones
through illness or accidents,
for all refugees and homeless people.

Silence

Lord, ever present,
help us to rejoice in your love and power.

We give thanks for the life of Jesus
and the offering to us of eternal life.
We pray for friends and loved ones who are departed from us.

Silence

Merciful Father,
accept these prayers
for the sake of your Son,
our Saviour Jesus Christ.
Amen.

Second Sunday of Christmas

YEAR C

God, we give you thanks for the New Year
and for all the opportunities that you offer us.
Blessed are you, Lord our God,
our Creator and our Redeemer.
Through your great love
your Son has shared in our joy and sorrow
and has delivered us from death.
Blessed are you, Lord God, giver of life and life eternal.

We give you thanks for all preachers of the word,
for translators of the Bible and for Bible publishers.
We pray for all who produce Bible guides,
commentaries and study notes.
We ask you to bless all who read and study the Scriptures.
We pray that we all may know the true and living Word
that is Christ our Lord.
May we know him as present in our lives
and with us always.

Silence

Come, Lord:
be known among us.

We pray for all who are involved in giving us information
through the daily news and newspapers,
for all who communicate with us
through the written or spoken word.
We remember all who suffer from deafness
or who are unable to speak.
We pray for all who have difficulty in communicating
and who are often misunderstood.

Silence

Come, Lord:
be known among us.

We give thanks for those who taught us to read and write.
We ask your blessing on our friends and our loved ones.
We pray that in this New Year
we may learn to be sensitive and caring for each other.

Silence

Come, Lord:
be known among us.

We pray for all who are fearful for their future,
those who are awaiting a doctor's diagnosis or an operation,
for all who are terminally ill.
We remember all who live in areas of war or natural disaster.
Lord, bless all who work in caring for others
and relieving their anxiety.

Silence

Come, Lord:
be known among us.

We ask your blessing upon our loved ones
who are now departed from us.
May they know newness of life in your kingdom.

Silence

Merciful Father,
accept these prayers
for the sake of your Son,
our Saviour Jesus Christ.
Amen.

The Epiphany

YEAR C

Blessed are you, Lord our God,
who by the leading of a star
brought seekers from other nations
to bow before the Christ child.
As they offered their gifts and their lives,
may we offer ourselves to you in love and adoration,
for you are the giver of life and life eternal.

Lord, as you led the wise men to the Christ,
lead us to know you and your love.
We pray for all who are seekers and pilgrims,
all who search for the meaning of life and for purpose.
We remember all who have lost touch with you
or who have no faith.
We pray for all who are caught up in materialism
or who are self-centred.
We ask that the Church may reach out to draw others to you.
We seek guidance for all bishops, priests and deacons.
May we all be led to a vision of you and your love.

Silence

Lord, guide us by your light
and bring us to your glory.

We give thanks for people of talent,
for men and women of vision,
for all who improve this world by their lives.
We ask your guidance upon all who influence the lives of others.
Bless all teachers, writers and those who influence us
through the press and broadcasting.
We ask you to guide all who are leaders of people or nations.

Silence

Lord, guide us by your light
and bring us to your glory.

We give thanks that Jesus lived in an ordinary home.
We ask your blessing upon our homes and loved ones.
May we know your presence and peace
in our lives and in our work.
We pray today for the lonely
and all who feel neglected or unwanted.
We remember all who suffer from violence or abuse
in their homes.

Silence

Lord, guide us by your light
and bring us to your glory.

Lord, we come with the sorrowing and sad people
of our world,
with all who live in fear or anxiety.
We pray for refugees and homeless people.
We remember all who are in pain or distress at this time.
May they all know that you love them and care for them.
We ask your blessing on all healers
and on relief organisations.

Silence

Lord, guide us by your light
and bring us to your glory.

We give thanks for the promise of eternal life
through the coming of your Son.
We rejoice in the fellowship of all your saints.
May our loved ones departed
know the fullness and joy of your eternal kingdom.

Silence

Merciful Father,
accept these prayers
for the sake of your Son,
our Saviour Jesus Christ.
Amen.

First Sunday of Epiphany
The Baptism of Christ
YEAR C

Blessed are you, Father, Son and Holy Spirit,
for you are ever with us and never leave us.
You are our Creator, Redeemer and Guide.
We come from you.
We belong to you.
We will return to you.
Blessed are you, Father, Son and Holy Spirit.

We give thanks for all your baptised and faithful people.
May we all rejoice in your presence and in your power.
We ask your blessing on all who are being prepared
for baptism, confirmation or ordination.
We pray for Church schools and Sunday schools,
for Bible classes and study groups.
We remember all who are seekers
and long to know you.

Silence

Hear us and help us,
Father, Son and Holy Spirit.

We pray for all who are beginning new work or new ventures.
We remember especially
any who are leaving home for the first time.
We ask your blessing upon those forming new relationships
and all who are newly married.
We pray for those who have the care of young families
and we remember any who are struggling at this time.

Silence

Hear us and help us,
Father, Son and Holy Spirit.

We give thanks for our own homes and loved ones.
We ask your blessing upon our parents and godparents,
upon our children and godchildren.
We pray for all who influence our lives
by their teaching or by their example.

Silence

Hear us and help us,
Father, Son and Holy Spirit.

We pray for all who are struggling with life,
those who are burdened with guilt or anger,
all who have memories that disturb them.
We remember all who are ill at home or in hospital,
especially any who feel lonely or unwanted.
We pray for all who have been taken into care this week.

Silence

Hear us and help us,
Father, Son and Holy Spirit.

We give thanks for all who have enriched our lives
by their goodness and care.
We pray for friends and loved ones who are departed from us.
May they know your love in the fullness of life eternal.

Silence

Merciful Father,
accept these prayers
for the sake of your Son,
our Saviour Jesus Christ.
Amen.

Second Sunday of Epiphany

YEAR C

Blessed are you, Lord our God,
giver of joy and life.
To you be praise and glory for ever.
In your presence is the fullness of joy.
With you is life and life eternal.

Lord God, strength of the weak
and light to all who walk in darkness,
help us to proclaim your saving power
not only in words but also by our lives.
Help us to reveal the joy of knowing you and your love.
We ask you to bless all preachers and teachers of the faith.
Guide all who study Scriptures
and all who are learning through the example of others.
We pray for all who are being prepared for Confirmation
at this time.

Silence

Lord of life and love,
renew and refresh us.

Lord, we pray for the world
and a right use of its resources.
We ask your blessing
upon any who are suffering from natural disasters,
upon those suffering from famine or flood.
We remember all whose resources are running low
and we pray for the world poor
and all who are without work or proper shelter.

Silence

Lord of life and love,
renew and refresh us.

We give thanks
for all who have supplied us with our daily needs,
for our homes and for our loved ones.
We ask your blessing on homes
that are suffering from great debt
or where the household is unable to cope
through various troubles.

Silence

Lord of life and love,
renew and refresh us.

We give thanks for our well-being
and we pray for all who are struggling at this time.
We remember those who are suffering
from physical disability or weakness,
all who are losing agility or mobility.
We pray for all who do not have the strength
to cope on their own.
We ask your blessing upon all who have been taken into care.

Silence

Lord of life and love,
renew and refresh us.

We give thanks for the resurrection of our Lord
and for the promise of life eternal.
We pray for our friends and loved ones departed
and ask that they may know
newness and fullness of life in your kingdom.
We rejoice in the fellowship of all your saints
and pray that we may share with them in glory.

Silence

Merciful Father,
accept these prayers
for the sake of your Son,
our Saviour Jesus Christ.
Amen.

Third Sunday of Epiphany

YEAR C

Blessed are you, Lord our God,
for by your Word all of life came into being.
You are the Creator, Redeemer and Sustainer of our world.
Today we rejoice in your presence and in your love.
May we heed your guidance through the Scriptures
and work for the coming of your kingdom.

We give thanks for all who preach and teach the Good News.
We ask your blessing upon all who translate
and produce the Scriptures,
upon those who provide Bible notes and commentaries.
We pray for all who study and read the Scriptures
and for any who meditate upon your word.
May we at all times be open to your presence and your love.

Silence

Lord, your word
gives life to us and to the world.

We give thanks for all who strive
to bring freedom and well-being to peoples and nations.
We remember any who are struggling
under oppression or captivity,
all who live in poverty or are homeless.
We pray for those who suffer from injustice or violence,
all who are victims of greed or insensitivity.
We ask you to bless the work of the United Nations
and all peacekeeping forces.

Silence

Lord, your word
gives life to us and to the world.

We give thanks for our homes
and for all who have cared for us and taught us.
Help us to be aware of your presence
in our homes and our loved ones.
We pray for any children who have been taken into care
or who are separated from their parents
due to illness or family problems.
We remember all who struggle with bad housing
or live in deprived areas.

Silence

Lord, your word
gives life to us and to the world.

We give thanks for our vision, our sight and insight.
We pray for all who suffer from blindness or restricted vision.
We remember those who have lost sight of you
or have no hope for the future.
We ask your blessing upon all who are ill,
who are in pain or in sorrow at this time.
We pray for all who are bereaved
and all who are lonely.

Silence

Lord, your word
gives life to us and to the world.

We give thanks for the gift of life and life eternal.
We rejoice in the fellowship of all your saints in glory.
We remember friends and loved ones
who are departed from us.
May they share with your saints
in that life and love which are eternal.

Silence

Merciful Father,
accept these prayers
for the sake of your Son,
our Saviour Jesus Christ.
Amen.

Fourth Sunday of Epiphany

(Also for use on the Feast of the Presentation)

YEAR C

By the mystery of the Word made flesh,
Lord, make yourself known to us.

By the coming of Christ, the Light of the World,
Lord, make yourself known to us.

By the birth of Jesus in Bethlehem,
Lord, make yourself known to us.

By his revealing to the shepherds and wise men,
Lord, make yourself known to us.

By his baptism, the voice from the cloud and the dove,
Lord, make yourself known to us.

By his changing water into wine,
Lord, make yourself known to us.

By his proclaiming of the Good News,
Lord, make yourself known to us.

God of light and love,
we remember before you
all who seek to proclaim the Good News.
We ask your blessing
upon all ministers of the word and the sacraments,
upon all who teach and preach in your name.
We pray for all who are striving
to bring the light of Christ to darkened lives.

Silence

Light of God,
shine upon us.

We remember all who live in darkness and in fear.
We pray for the persecuted and the homeless,
for all who are captives or suffer from war or terrorism.
We ask your blessing
upon all who are anxious for their lives.

Silence

Light of God,
shine upon us.

We pray for all who suffer from blindness
or impairment of their sight,
for those who suffer from river blindness.
We ask you to bless all who seek to relieve their suffering
and to restore sight.
We pray for any who have lost vision of you and your love.

Silence

Light of God,
shine upon us.

We remember all who are in the valley of the shadow of death,
all who have passed beyond it to light and life eternal.
We pray for our loved ones departed from us.
May we all come to rejoice in the fullness of your kingdom.

Silence

Merciful Father,
accept these prayers
for the sake of your Son,
our Saviour Jesus Christ.
Amen.

Proper 1

Sunday between 3 and 9 February inclusive
(if earlier than the Second Sunday before Lent)

YEAR C

Blessed are you, Lord our God,
for you have called us to know you,
to love you and to serve you.
We rejoice in your presence
and in your love for us.
Blessed are you, Father, Son and Holy Spirit.

We give you thanks, O God,
for all who have served you faithfully throughout the ages.
We thank you especially today
for the prophet Isaiah and for the disciples.
We ask your blessing upon all who are called
to preach the word and to celebrate the sacraments.
We pray for theological colleges and their students
and for all your people in their various vocations.

Silence

Father, as you have called us,
give us the power to serve you.

We ask your blessing upon all who feel drained
of resources or energy.
We remember those who are handicapped
by poverty or by the prejudice of others.
We pray for people who feel they have lost their way
or who have been cast aside by society.
We remember the street children of the world
and those who live in slums.

Silence

Father, as you have called us,
give us the power to serve you.

We give thanks that you have called us to know you
and we pray that we may live to your glory.
May our homes and our relationships reflect our love for you.
We remember before you
homes where there is tension or violence
or where there is neglect
and a lack of respect for each other.

Silence

Father, as you have called us,
give us the power to serve you.

We pray for all who are called to the healing professions.
We ask your blessing on doctors and surgeons,
on nurses and on ambulance crews.
We pray for all who are ill at home or in hospital
and we remember those who are unable to cope on their own.

Silence

Father, as you have called us,
give us the power to serve you.

We give thanks that you have called us to life eternal.
We remember in your presence
friends and loved ones who are departed from us.
May they share with your saints
in the glory of your kingdom.

Silence

Merciful Father,
accept these prayers
for the sake of your Son,
our Saviour Jesus Christ.
Amen.

Proper 2

Sunday between 10 and 16 February inclusive
(if earlier than the Second Sunday before Lent)

YEAR C

Blessed are you, Lord our God;
in your presence are joy and peace.
You never leave us or forsake us,
so help us to rejoice in you,
in your love and in your saving power.
Blessed are you, Father, Son and Holy Spirit.

God, we give you thanks
for all who show a radiant faith,
for those who show that in your presence
is the fullness of joy.
Help us also to show the joy and wonder of your love
and to find happiness in your service.
We pray for all who preach the word
and administer the sacraments,
that they may reveal the delight of knowing you.

Silence

Lord, bless us with your presence
and the joy of knowing your love.

We pray for all who are homeless, hungry or unemployed.
We remember the deprived and poor peoples of our world.
We ask your blessing upon all who suffer
from violence or from war.
May they all know the joy of your love
and that you value each of them.

Silence

Lord, bless us with your presence
and the joy of knowing your love.

We give thanks for our homes and our loved ones.
We remember all who have enriched our lives
by their love or their friendship.
We pray for homes where there is little love or joy
or where there is neglect or abuse.

Silence

Lord, bless us with your presence
and the joy of knowing your love.

We give thanks for all who work as healers
and ask your blessing upon all who are doctors, nurses
or part of the caring and healing professions.
We remember all who are ill at home or in hospital,
all who have been injured
or rushed into hospital this week.
We pray for those who have lost loved ones and friends.

Silence

Lord, bless us with your presence
and the joy of knowing your love.

We rejoice in the gift of eternal life
and we pray for our loved ones departed.
May they share in the happiness of your saints in glory.

Silence

Merciful Father,
accept these prayers
for the sake of your Son,
our Saviour Jesus Christ.
Amen.

Proper 3

Sunday between 17 and 23 February inclusive
(if earlier than the Second Sunday before Lent)

YEAR C

Blessed are you, good and generous God,
for you give us life and all that we have.
Help us to be as generous and forgiving
as you are with us.
May we appreciate all that you have given us
and all that you have done for us throughout our lives.
Blessed are you, Father, Son and Holy Spirit.

We give thanks for all who have shown your ways
by their love and generosity.
We give thanks for all who give their lives in your service.
We remember today all who seek to maintain worship
in dangerous or difficult places.
We pray for prison chaplains and prison visitors.
We remember those who are persecuted
or imprisoned for their faith.
We pray for all who strive to love
in areas of hatred and resentment.

Silence

God of goodness and love,
give us a loving and courageous heart.

We ask your blessing
upon all who seek to bring peace and unity to our world.
We pray for the work of the Red Cross and all relief agencies.
We remember all who are suffering
from natural disasters or war at this time.
We pray especially for those who have lost loved ones
or are separated from them.

Silence

God of goodness and love,
give us a loving and courageous heart.

We give thanks for the protection and love of our own homes.
We ask your blessing upon all who are homeless
or who have been taken into care.
We pray for all who are lonely
and those who are finding it difficult to cope on their own.

Silence

God of goodness and love,
give us a loving and courageous heart.

We give thanks for our own well-being,
that in you, Lord, we are forgiven and freed to live life to the full.
We pray for all who are prisoners
of their own greed or unforgiving hearts.
We remember all who are consumed with rage or violence.
We pray for all who are ill at home or in hospital,
especially those who are not at peace with themselves.

Silence

God of goodness and love,
give us a loving and courageous heart.

We give thanks for the gift of life and life eternal.
We remember in your presence the generosity of your saints
and of our benefactors who are departed from us.
May our loved ones who are gone from our sight
rejoice with them in your glorious kingdom.

Silence

Merciful Father,
accept these prayers
for the sake of your Son,
our Saviour Jesus Christ.
Amen.

Second Sunday before Lent

YEAR C

Blessed are you, Lord our God,
for you created the world out of chaos
and when chaos seeks to overwhelm us
you offer us your presence and your peace.
You are ever with us in the storms of life
and we know you as our Saviour.
Blessed are you, Father, Son and Holy Spirit.

Lord, your ship the Church is often buffeted
by storms of oppression and violence.
At all times may we affirm your abiding presence
and your lasting peace.
We remember all who are struggling with their faith,
all who do not know you or love you.
May your Church bring to them
the knowledge of your love
and of your Almighty Power.

Silence

Holy and strong One,
grant us your peace.

We give thanks for all who seek
to bring your peace to the world.
We pray for the work of the United Nations
and peacekeeping forces.
We remember all who are caught up
in the violence of war or tyranny.
We ask your blessing
upon those who are being overwhelmed by life,
upon all who feel they cannot survive on their own.

Silence

Holy and strong One,
grant us your peace.

We pray for our homes and our loved ones.
May we here reveal your peace in our dealings
and in our relationships.
We ask your blessing on homes
that are sinking into deep debt
or where families are unable to cope with each other.

Silence

Holy and strong One,
grant us your peace.

We give thanks for our peace of mind
and we pray for all who are disturbed or distressed.
We remember those who have had a traumatic experience
and those who have suffered from betrayal or violence.
We pray for all who are not at peace
with themselves or with others.

Silence

Holy and strong One,
grant us your peace.

We rejoice that nothing can separate us
from the love of God in Christ Jesus,
that through him life is eternal.
We pray for friends and loved ones
who have passed beyond the storms of life:
may they rejoice in the joy of your presence
and in your everlasting peace.

Silence

Merciful Father,
accept these prayers
for the sake of your Son,
our Saviour Jesus Christ.
Amen.

Sunday before Lent

YEAR C

Blessed are you, Lord our God,
for you have revealed yourself
through Moses and the prophets.
You have made yourself known to us through your saints
but, above all, you show us your glory
in the face of our Lord Jesus Christ.
Blessed are you, God, for ever.

We give thanks for men and women of vision,
for all who have shown us of you and your love.
We ask that your Church may continue
to show forth your glory in the world.
We seek your blessing upon preachers of the word
and ministers of the sacraments,
upon all who teach and speak in your name.

Silence

Wonderful God,
reveal in us your glory.

We give thanks for artists and craftspeople,
for all who give us a vision of beauty and wonder.
We ask your blessing upon all architects and planners,
upon councils and governments,
that they might keep a clear vision of what is good for our world.
We pray for all who make decisions
that will affect the future of the human race.

Silence

Wonderful God,
reveal in us your glory.

We give thanks for those who have cared for us and taught us.
We ask your blessing upon our homes,
our friends and families.
We pray for all homes where there is little sense of love
or where there is neglect or abuse.
We ask you to guide all who have the care of families,
who are struggling with their relationships.

Silence

Wonderful God,
reveal in us your glory.

We give thanks for all who have made discoveries in medicine
and all who are responsible for the care of human life.
We pray for all doctors and nurses
and our own local health centres.
We ask your blessing upon all who are suffering at this time,
especially any who feel
they no longer have any value or influence.

Silence

Wonderful God,
reveal in us your glory.

We give thanks for all who have witnessed
to your love and saving power.
We rejoice in the fellowship of all your saints
and pray that our loved ones departed may share with them
in the fullness of your eternal kingdom.

Silence

Merciful Father,
accept these prayers
for the sake of your Son,
our Saviour Jesus Christ.
Amen.

First Sunday of Lent

YEAR C

Blessed are you, Lord our God,
for you never leave us or forsake us.
When we wander away from you,
you keep with us.
When we turn our backs on you,
you wait patiently until we turn again.
You are a loving and a forgiving God.
Blessed are you, Father, Son and Holy Spirit.

God, we thank you for our talents and abilities
and for all the people who help us to achieve in life.
We ask your blessing upon all who set high ideals and hopes
for our society and the world.
We pray for all who are striving to improve their lives
and the communities in which they live.
We give thanks for the Church and its ministers
and ask your guidance and grace to be upon it.
We remember all who are struggling
against evil and wickedness at this time.

Silence

Lord, as you forgive and offer us newness of life,
help us to forgive.

We remember in your presence
all who have given their lives in the service and care of others.
We pray for those who seek to keep law and order,
all who influence the minds of the young
and all who shape our society by their actions.
We ask your blessing especially
on those who stand against evil
at the risk of their own lives or well-being.

Silence

Lord, as you forgive and offer us newness of life,
help us to forgive.

We give thanks for our homes and our loved ones.
Lord, may we make our homes fit for your presence
and able to reveal your love.
We pray for all who harbour anger, resentment
or hatred in their hearts.
May they learn the joy and freedom
of forgiveness and mercy.

Silence

Lord, as you forgive and offer us newness of life,
help us to forgive.

Lord God, we thank you for your loving kindness towards us.
We pray for all who are caught up in crime,
in violence or in drugs,
for all who have lost hold on a good way of life.
May they discover a new way and a new freedom in you.
We pray for victims of crime
or any who have been injured through the carelessness of others.
We remember also all who are ill at home or in hospital,
especially those known to us.

Silence

Lord, as you forgive and offer us newness of life,
help us to forgive.

We rejoice in the witness of the saints
who sought to live holy and righteous lives.
We pray for our loved ones departed:
may they know newness of life in your kingdom
and enjoy your presence and love for ever.

Silence

Merciful Father,
accept these prayers
for the sake of your Son,
our Saviour Jesus Christ.
Amen.

Second Sunday of Lent

YEAR C

Blessed are you, Lord our God,
for you give us life and promise us life eternal.
In your Son you have shown us
the joy and the fullness of your kingdom.
Throughout our lives you offer us
your light and your salvation.
Blessed are you, Father, Son and Holy Spirit.

Father, as we give you thanks
for our freedom and ability to choose
we pray for all who are being persecuted for their faith.
We remember those who live in homes
where faith is discouraged or scorned.
We ask your blessing
on all who are struggling with their faith
or who are tempted to turn their back on you.

Silence

Lord, we come to you:
you are our light and salvation.

We rejoice in the good things of our land.
We pray that justice and freedom will be for all peoples.
We remember today all who are imprisoned
for speaking out against evil
or for resisting a corrupt regime.
We also pray today for the peace of Jerusalem.

Silence

Lord, we come to you:
you are our light and salvation.

We give thanks for our homes
and for those who have provided us
with love and security.
We ask your blessing upon our families and our friends.
We pray for homes where there is division and violence.
We remember especially today
children who are taken into care
and children who are in danger.

Silence

Lord, we come to you:
you are our light and salvation.

We pray for all who work in the healing professions,
all who do research in medicines
and all who care for ill people.
We pray for friends and loved ones who are ill
at home or in hospital.
We pray especially today for . . .
We ask your blessing upon all whose illness finds no cure.

Silence

Lord, we come to you:
you are our light and salvation.

We give thanks for the gift of eternal life
and we pray for friends and loved ones
who are departed from us.
May we rejoice with them
in the fellowship of all your saints.

Silence

Merciful Father
accept these prayers
for the sake of your Son,
our Saviour Jesus Christ.
Amen.

Third Sunday of Lent

YEAR C

Blessed are you, Lord our God,
for you are our Creator.
You have made us out of your love and for your love.
You have created us to enjoy this earth
and to bring forth the fruits of the Spirit.
Blessed are you, Father, Son and Holy Spirit.

We give thanks for your Church throughout the world,
that it is a place of shelter and security,
that it offers sanctuary and peace to many.
May the Church be a place where talents are developed
and your purpose fulfilled.
May we each show in our lives the fruits of the Spirit
in love, joy and peace.
We pray especially for any who are struggling with their faith
and for those who are learning to turn to new ways.

Silence

Lord, you are our helper:
your hand holds us fast.

We thank you for all who provide us
with food and the essentials of life.
We ask your blessing upon all who grow crops
and care for sheep and cattle,
and upon fishermen.
We pray today for all who are unemployed
or have been made redundant,
all who are unable to work through illness.
May they still know they have a purpose in life
and that they are useful members of our communities.

Silence

Lord, you are our helper:
your hand holds us fast.

We give thanks for our parents and all they have done for us.
May we be useful members of our home and community.
We pray for all who are struggling with debt
or with division within the family.
We ask your blessing upon our loved ones and friends.

Silence

Lord, you are our helper:
your hand holds us fast.

We remember before you, O Lord,
all who feel that they are unwanted or rejected.
We pray for those who suffer from a disability
and those who are unable to cope on their own
through illness or through becoming weak and frail.
May they know they are respected and loved members
of our communities.
Lord, give them courage and hope in their troubles.

Silence

Lord, you are our helper:
your hand holds us fast.

We rejoice in the gift of eternal life.
Help us to live that life as fully as we can now
to your glory and to the benefit of others.
We remember all who have improved our world
by their lives and their attention.
We give thanks for all your saints
and we ask you to bless our loved ones
who have departed from us.

Silence

Merciful Father,
accept these prayers
for the sake of your Son,
our Saviour Jesus Christ.
Amen.

Fourth Sunday of Lent

Mothering Sunday

YEAR C

(Let families pray the intercessions today. The first part is devised for younger children to pray. Remember they need rehearsing and need to be heard.)

For our parents and the love that they give to us,
God, we thank you
and we praise you.

For our mother's love and care,
God, we thank you
and we praise you.

For our father's love and protection,
God, we thank you
and we praise you.

For the love we share with our brothers and sisters,
God, we thank you
and we praise you.

For our homes and all that you give us,
God, we thank you
and we praise you.

We pray for Mother Church that helps us to grow in the faith,
for our clergy and all who minister to us and care for us,
for all who help us to know and love God.

Silence

Loving Father,
hear us and help us.

We remember today all homeless peoples,
all who are separated from their loved ones
through war or troubles.
We pray for any who are taken into care,
whether they are young or old.
We ask your blessing upon all who have lost loved ones this year
and upon all who are feeling lonely or unwanted.

Silence

Loving Father,
hear us and help us.

We give thanks for our own homes
and ask your blessing upon our family and friends.
We ask you especially to bless our mother at this time.
We pray for mothers throughout the world;
may they never be taken for granted
and always be respected.

Silence

Loving Father,
hear us and help us.

We pray for all who are ill at home or in hospital.
We remember families where the mother is ill
or where she is tending an ill child.
We ask your blessing upon families
where there is poverty or the inability to cope.

Silence

Loving Father,
hear us and help us.

We give thanks, O God, for your loving care
and we ask your blessing upon all our loved ones and friends
who have departed this life and are at peace in your kingdom.

Silence

Merciful Father,
accept these prayers
for the sake of your Son,
our Saviour Jesus Christ.
Amen.

Fifth Sunday of Lent

YEAR C

Blessed are you, Lord our God,
for you love us with an everlasting love.
You have given your only Son for our salvation
and to bring us to eternal life.
Blessed are you, Lord God, now and for ever.

Father, we give you thanks for all who have given their lives
in love and service of humankind.
We remember today all who quietly live sacrificially
so that others may enjoy the fullness of life.
We ask you to bless all who risk their lives
to bring the Good News to others.
We pray for any who feel that their ministry
is a lonely and unrewarding task.

Silence

Help us, Lord, to serve you,
to give and not to count the cost.

We give thanks for all who have offered their talents and time
without questioning the cost.
We pray for all who work in the emergency services.
We ask you to bless all who are seeking
to relieve poverty and oppression in the world.

Silence

Help us, Lord, to serve you,
to give and not to count the cost.

We praise you for our loved ones
who have enriched our lives by their care and goodness.
We ask your blessing upon our families and friends,
upon our teachers and all who have been our benefactors.
We pray for all who feel neglected and unwanted.

Silence

Help us, Lord, to serve you,
to give and not to count the cost.

We give thanks for all you have given us, O God.
We remember in your presence
all who are suffering,
all who are being persecuted,
all who are oppressed.
May we help where we can
to ease their pain or their troubles.

Silence

Help us, Lord, to serve you,
to give and not to count the cost.

We give thanks that through the love of Christ
and his offering of himself on the cross
you have opened to us the way to life eternal.
We ask your blessing upon your saints
and upon all our loved ones departed.
May we rejoice with them
in your love and in your kingdom.

Silence

Merciful Father,
accept these prayers
for the sake of your Son,
our Saviour Jesus Christ.
Amen.

Palm Sunday

YEAR C

Blessed are you, Lord our God, for you have redeemed us
by the offering of your Son upon the cross.
Through his death you destroy death
and open to us the kingdom of heaven.
As we seek to welcome Jesus into our lives
with cries of 'Hosanna',
and as we walk the way of the cross,
keep us ever mindful of your love and your peace.
Blessed are you, Father, with the Son and the Holy Spirit.

Lord God, we thank you
for the coming of Christ into the world
and sharing in our troubles.
We rejoice in your saving power and in the promise of life eternal.
We pray for all who seek to walk the way of the cross this week.
We remember pilgrims in Jerusalem
and all who keep this Holy Week.
We ask your blessing upon all Christians
who are facing persecution and rejection at this time.

Silence

Give thanks to the Lord for he is good;
his mercy endures for ever.

We pray for the peace of the world,
that the nations of the world may come
to find peace through the Prince of Peace.
We remember all who are suffering
through acts of violence and tyranny,
all who are being ill-treated,
the scorned and rejected of the world.

Silence

Give thanks to the Lord for he is good;
his mercy endures for ever.

We give thanks for the love of families and friends
and we ask your blessing upon their lives.
We remember today the homeless
and all who are finding it difficult to cope on their own.
We pray for all who live on the streets
and have no one to care for them.

Silence

Give thanks to the Lord for he is good;
his mercy endures for ever.

We give thanks for the loyalty of friends
and we pray for all who have been betrayed
by friends or loved ones.
We ask your blessing on those who are deeply hurt
by the actions of others.
We pray for all who harbour hatred and resentment
and ask that they might find the power to forgive.

Silence

Give thanks to the Lord for he is good;
his mercy endures for ever.

As we remember the death and passion of our Lord,
we rejoice in his victory.
We pray for loved ones who have departed from us.
We remember all who have been bereaved recently
and all who have lost their lives
through accidents or acts of violence.
May they know of your love and the joy of your kingdom.

Silence

Merciful Father,
accept these prayers
for the sake of your Son,
our Saviour Jesus Christ.
Amen.

Easter Day

YEAR C

Blessed are you, Lord our God.
On the first Easter Day you raised your Son, Jesus Christ,
triumphant over death, sin and evil.
In his death you have destroyed death
and in his rising to life you have opened to us
the kingdom of heaven.
Blessed are you, Father, Son and Holy Spirit.

With the whole Church
throughout the world and in heaven
we rejoice,
for Christ is risen.
Let every Christian rejoice,
let every heart rejoice,
for Christ is risen.
We ask your blessing this day
on all who are celebrating the resurrection.
We pray especially for groups that are persecuted
or oppressed because of their faith.
We remember also all who doubt the Good News
and all who are seekers.

Silence

Jesus, stand among us
in your risen power.

We remember today all who are struggling with life.
We pray for the world's poor, refugees
and all who are used as work slaves.
We ask your blessing upon all who are losing heart
or who feel discouraged and despondent.

Silence

Jesus, stand among us
in your risen power.

We give thanks for those who taught us the faith
and introduced us to the living Lord.
We pray for schools and Sunday Schools,
for all teachers of Religious Education.
We ask you to bless us with your presence
in our homes and in our work.

Silence

Jesus, stand among us
in your risen power.

We pray for all who are terminally ill,
for all who are in a hospice or in care.
We pray also for their loved ones in this time of anxiety.
We remember those who have been bereaved this year,
especially all who are left on their own
and feel lonely or unable to cope.
Lord, bless all whose powers are failing
with your love and strength.

Silence

Jesus, stand among us
in your risen power.

We rejoice in your triumph over death
and we pray for all your saints
and our loved ones who have departed this life.
May they rejoice with us this Easter Day
in the fullness of life eternal.

Silence

Merciful Father,
accept these prayers
for the sake of your Son,
our Saviour Jesus Christ.
Amen.

Second Sunday of Easter

YEAR C

Blessed are you, God and Father of our Lord Jesus Christ.
To you be praise and glory for ever.
Alleluia.
By the raising of your Son from the dead
you have opened to us the way to eternal life.
You have given us an everlasting joy and a deep peace
through bringing us to know the risen Christ.
Blessed are you, Father, Son and Holy Spirit.

We give thanks for your faithful people
throughout the world,
for the fellowship of all believers.
We ask you to bless all who preach and teach
the reality of the resurrection.
We pray for all who are struggling with doubt
and for all who are seeking a relationship with you.

Silence

Risen Christ, be known among us
and give us your peace.

We give thanks for the gift of peace
and pray there may be peace in our hearts,
in our homes and in the whole world.
We remember areas where there is warfare and strife.
We pray for all who are not at peace
with themselves or with you.
We ask you to bless all who are working
for peace in our world.

Silence

Risen Christ, be known among us
and give us your peace.

Lord Jesus, as we rejoice
in your risen presence in an earthly home,
make yourself known to us in our homes,
in our fellowship
and in the breaking of the bread.
Lord, teach us to be at home with you in our homes.
May our homes be where your presence is known.

Silence

Risen Christ, be known among us
and give us your peace.

We give thanks for the new hope and courage
that is ours through the resurrection.
We pray for all who are discouraged
or without hope at this time.
We remember those who are seriously ill
and any who are facing death.
We pray for those who are tending the ill
and any who are anxious about loved ones.

Silence

Risen Christ, be known among us
and give us your peace.

We rejoice in the defeat of death
by the resurrection of our Lord.
We pray for all who have given their lives
in the service of humankind,
all martyrs and saints.
We remember our loved ones departed
and ask that they may rejoice
in the fullness of life eternal.

Silence

Merciful Father,
accept these prayers
for the sake of your Son,
our Saviour Jesus Christ.
Amen.

Third Sunday of Easter

YEAR C

Blessed are you, Lord our God,
for you have called us out of darkness
into the glorious light of your presence;
you fill our emptiness with the richness of your love.
We rejoice in the power of the resurrection
and in your gift of eternal life.
Blessed are you, Father, Son and Holy Spirit.

Lord, we thank you for calling us to follow you
and to share in your outreach to all peoples.
We ask your blessing upon all who go out to preach the word,
upon all pastors and shepherds of your flock.
Give us all the wisdom to follow in your steps
and to bring others to know and love you.
We pray for all who are involved in mission
and in spreading the Good News
through teaching and example.

Silence

Hear us, O Lord, and have mercy upon us;
O Lord, be our helper.

We give thanks that you give us strength and courage
through your presence.
We pray for all whose work
appears to be meaningless or fruitless.
We remember those who are virtually slaves
and work for a very small income.
We ask your blessing upon all who have been made redundant
and all who are unemployed.

Silence

Hear us, O Lord, and have mercy upon us;
O Lord, be our helper.

We praise you, O God,
for the love and protection of our homes.
We ask your blessing upon each of our loved ones,
our families and friends.
We pray for homes where there is little joy or love.
We remember all who are struggling with their relationships
and all who feel lonely or unwanted.

Silence

Hear us, O Lord, and have mercy upon us;
O Lord, be our helper.

Lord, we ask your blessing
upon all who are discouraged or despondent at this time,
upon all who feel that life is not worthwhile.
May they know of your love and your presence.
We pray for all who are ill at home or in hospital,
all who are fearful of the future
and anxious about their loved ones.

Silence

Hear us, O Lord, and have mercy upon us;
O Lord, be our helper.

We give thanks for the risen Lord,
ever-present and welcoming us to the fullness of eternal life.
We pray for our loved ones who are departed from us;
may they share with your saints
in the joy of your kingdom.

Silence

Merciful Father,
accept these prayers
for the sake of your Son,
our Saviour Jesus Christ.
Amen.

Fourth Sunday of Easter

YEAR C

Blessed are you, Father, Son and Holy Spirit.
Through Jesus Christ
you have broken the power of sin and death
and opened the kingdom of heaven to all believers.
Through Christ the Good Shepherd
you lead us from darkness into your glorious light;
you lead us from death to life eternal.
We rejoice that nothing can snatch us from your hand.
Blessed are you, One God now and for ever.

Father, we give you thanks and praise
for Jesus the Good Shepherd.
Help us to hear his voice and to follow him.
We pray for all who share his pastoral ministry,
all preachers of the word and ministers of the sacraments.
We ask your blessing upon all who go out in home visits,
all carers, doctors and nurses and home helpers.
We remember especially
those who reach out to the outcasts and rejected.

Silence

Good Shepherd, guide us
and help us always.

We give thanks for all who seek
to bring peace and unity to our world.
We ask your blessing upon all shepherds,
farmers and fishermen and all who work in agriculture
or to provide us with food and clothing.
We ask you to guide all who have the care of young people,
all teachers, youth leaders and social workers.

Silence

Good Shepherd, guide us
and help us always.

Father, we give thanks
for all who have cared for us and provided for us.
We pray especially for parents and loved ones,
for our families and friends.
We pray for those who have taught us the faith
and been examples to us,
and we ask your blessing
upon all who are still our guides and helpers.

Silence

Good Shepherd, guide us
and help us always.

Father, we pray for all who have lost their way in life.
We remember those who have lost faith
in themselves, in others or in their God.
We pray for all who are finding life desperate
and are disillusioned or fearful.
We ask you to comfort and bless all who are struggling
with illness or problems that they cannot solve
and those who feel unable to find help or hope.

Silence

Good Shepherd, guide us
and help us always.

We rejoice that the Good Shepherd gives us life eternal
and that nothing can separate us
from the love of God in Christ Jesus.
We join with the fellowship of the saints
and our loved ones departed to praise you.
We commend them and ourselves to your unfailing love.

Silence

Merciful Father,
accept these prayers
for the sake of your Son,
our Saviour Jesus Christ.
Amen.

Fifth Sunday of Easter

YEAR C

Blessed are you, Father, Son and Holy Spirit,
our Creator, Saviour and Inspirer.
We give thanks for your love and glory
revealed in the death and resurrection of Jesus.
We rejoice in his love for us
and seek to be his friends always.
Blessed are you, One God for ever.

We give thanks for the faithfulness of your disciples
and the love of your saints throughout the ages.
May your glory be revealed through your Church today.
We ask your blessing upon all who proclaim
your love and your saving power,
upon all who are seeking
to bring reconciliation and peace to the world.
We ask you to bless
all who translate and publish the Scriptures
and all who reach out in mission.

Silence

Lord, in your love,
renew and restore us.

We praise you, Lord, for your renewing powers
and we ask your blessing upon areas
that have been marred and spoiled by greed or war.
We pray for all who live in deprived or slum areas.
We remember those who have lost their homes
through debt or violence.
We remember all who are refugees or victims of terror.

Silence

Lord, in your love,
renew and restore us.

We give thanks for all who have been our friends
and helpers throughout our lives.
We ask your blessing upon our homes and our loved ones.
We pray for friends whom we have not seen for a while
and for all who share our daily lives.
We remember any who are lonely
and feel unloved or unwanted.

Silence

Lord, in your love,
renew and restore us.

Lord, we remember your suffering
and we pray for all who have been betrayed with a kiss
or deserted by friends.
We remember those whose relationships are breaking down
and those separated from their loved ones
due to illness or infirmity.
We pray for all who are suffering at this time
either at home or in hospital.

Silence

Lord, in your love,
renew and restore us.

We give thanks that by your death you destroyed death
and by your rising to life again have restored us to eternal life.
We remember in your presence the saints known and unknown
who have been loyal to you to the end.
We ask that our friends and loved ones departed
may share with them in the glory of your kingdom.

Silence

Merciful Father,
accept these prayers
for the sake of your Son,
our Saviour Jesus Christ.
Amen.

Sixth Sunday of Easter

YEAR C

Blessed are you, Father, Son and Holy Spirit.
In your presence is the fullness of joy.
You are our light and our salvation.
In you is our peace,
the peace that the world cannot give.
Blessed are you, one God now and for ever.

Lord God, we give you thanks for your peace
that you offer to us and to all people.
May your church be a true instrument of your peace,
bringing love where there has been hatred,
and fellowship where there has been division.
May your peace be seen in our actions
and within our community.
We pray for all who are not at peace
with themselves, with each other or with you.

Silence

Good and gracious God,
give us your peace.

We pray for the world
divided by strife and suffering from disunity.
Help us to know the peace we should accept,
the peace we should give
and the peace we need to forgo.
We pray for the United Nations
and for peacekeeping forces throughout our world.
We remember all who are suffering
from war or political unrest at this time.

Silence

Good and gracious God,
give us your peace.

We thank you for our homes,
for their comfort and their security.
We pray for homes where your peace is not easily found.
We remember families divided by hatred and violence,
all who have little or no peace in their hearts or lives.
We pray for all who are suffering
from stress or tension within their relationships.

Silence

Good and gracious God,
give us your peace.

Lord, we remember all disturbed and distressed people,
all who have suffered from traumatic events
or who are troubled in spirit.
We pray for all who are exhausted or depressed at this time,
for all who can find no rest.
We ask your blessing upon all who are ill or in pain,
upon those in hospital or being cared for at home.

Silence

Good and gracious God,
give us your peace.

We give thanks that through your love we have life eternal.
We pray for friends and loved ones departed;
may they rejoice in your presence and in your peace.
We commend ourselves and your whole world
to your peace and your unfailing love.

Silence

Merciful Father,
accept these prayers
for the sake of your Son,
our Saviour Jesus Christ.
Amen.

Ascension Day

YEAR C

Blessed are you, Father, Son and Holy Spirit.
Through the mighty acts of our Lord
you have offered us a share in your love
and in your heavenly kingdom;
you have opened for us the gate of heaven.
As Christ has ascended,
may we, in heart and mind, ascend
and know his presence with us now and always.

With your whole Church
we rejoice and praise you for the Ascension.
In your coming down and ascending
you have raised our humanity to the heights.
May the Church ever proclaim you
as King and present in your world.
We pray for all who are struggling with their faith
and for all who do not know you;
may they come to know you, your love and your peace.

Silence

Good and gracious God,
grant us a glimpse of your glory.

We give thanks for the glorious freedom
of the children of God.
We remember all who are captives at this time,
all who are stuck in a way of life
from which they would like to escape.
We pray for those caught up in drugs and in vice,
all who have fallen into wickedness and sin.
We ask your blessing upon all who are seeking
to help the outcasts and poor of society.

Silence

Good and gracious God,
grant us a glimpse of your glory.

Lord, may your love be known
in our hearts and in our homes.
We pray for all who seek to raise our spirits
through music, art and recreation.
We pray for writers and actors.
We pray for all who give hospitality
through hotels and bed-and-breakfast accommodation.
We remember all who are without a home or shelter.

Silence

Good and gracious God,
grant us a glimpse of your glory.

We give thanks for our salvation
and we pray for all
who have fallen into sickness, weariness, or sorrow.
We ask your blessing upon those in hospital
and those who are being cared for by loved ones at home.
We pray for all who feel down and depressed.

Silence

Good and gracious God,
grant us a glimpse of your glory.

Lord, as you have ascended
let us look to you and the hope of life eternal.
Bless with your love
all our friends and dear ones departed.
May we share with them one day
in your kingdom and glory.

Silence

Merciful Father,
accept these prayers
for the sake of your Son,
our Saviour Jesus Christ.
Amen.

Seventh Sunday of Easter

YEAR C

Blessed are you, Lord our God.
To you be praise and glory for ever.
You have become one with us
in taking our humanity into the Godhead.
Now we are one with you
and share in your love and glory.
May we rejoice that we dwell in you
and you are in us
this day and for ever.
Blessed are you, Father, Son and Holy Spirit.

Let us rejoice with the whole Church
in the Ascension of our Lord.
May the lives of all who are Christian
reveal your presence and your love to others.
Bless all preachers of the word
and ministers of the sacraments.
We pray for all who lead retreats and quiet days,
all who teach Religious Education
and all who are training in theological colleges.

Silence

Risen and ascended Lord,
hear us and help us.

We give thanks for men and women of vision.
We pray for all who are doing scientific research,
all who are exploring into the depths and mysteries of creation.
May we learn to use all new discoveries with wisdom
and with respect for the earth and all its creatures.

Silence

Risen and ascended Lord,
hear us and help us.

We give thanks for the love we have received
at home and through our friends.
We ask your blessing
upon all who seek to strengthen family life
and to improve the surroundings
of those who live in deprived or run-down areas.
We pray for any who are tempted by drugs or vice,
that they may have a vision of a better way of living.

Silence

Risen and ascended Lord,
hear us and help us.

We remember all who are struggling to survive.
We pray for the world poor, the homeless and the war-torn.
We ask your blessing upon all who are refugees
or who suffer from famine.
We pray for all who are ill and unable to enjoy life to the full.

Silence

Risen and ascended Lord,
hear us and help us.

We give thanks that we have a great High Priest
who has entered into the heavens,
even Jesus our Lord.
May the faithful departed,
in fellowship with all your saints,
rejoice with the ascended Lord in glory.

Silence

Merciful Father,
accept these prayers
for the sake of your Son,
our Saviour Jesus Christ.
Amen.

Pentecost

YEAR C

Blessed are you, Lord our God.
To you be praise and glory for ever.
Your Spirit moved over the face of the deep at the beginning
to bring order out of chaos and light and life into the world.
Pour your Spirit into our hearts
and kindle in us the fire of your love,
that we may reveal your power in our lives
and walk in the joy of your presence.
Blessed are you, Father, Son and Holy Spirit.

Come, Holy Spirit, fill our lives
which without you would be dull and cold.
Fill our Church which without you would be an empty shrine.
We ask you to guide and strengthen all who preach the word,
all who teach the faith.
We pray for all who are preparing
for Confirmation or for Ordination,
for all who are seeking to grow in the faith
and in a relationship with you.

Silence

Come, Holy Spirit, fill our hearts:
renew and refresh your creation.

We give thanks for all who are inspired and guided by you.
We ask your blessing upon all artists, musicians,
writers and craftspeople.
We pray for all who influence the minds of others
through broadcasting or through their example of living.
We remember today
all who live in deprived or depressing surroundings.

Silence

Come, Holy Spirit, fill our hearts:
renew and refresh your creation.

We give thanks for the coming of the Spirit
and the filling of an earthly home.
We ask your blessing upon our homes and our relationships.
We pray that our friendships enrich each other
and help us to be more aware of you.
We pray for all who are taken into care
and all who lack the love of a stable home.

Silence

Come, Holy Spirit, fill our hearts:
renew and refresh your creation.

We remember all exhausted peoples,
the world-weary, the depressed and the discouraged.
We pray for all who despair
and all who feel they can no longer cope with life.
We ask your blessing upon friends and loved ones who are ill
and upon all who have been involved in accidents this week.

Silence

Come, Holy Spirit, fill our hearts:
renew and refresh your creation.

We give thanks for the gift of the Spirit
and the promise of eternal life.
We remember all who have served you faithfully
and are now at rest in your kingdom.
We pray for loved ones and friends
who are departed from us,
that they may rejoice in life eternal.

Silence

Merciful Father,
accept these prayers
for the sake of your Son,
our Saviour Jesus Christ.
Amen.

Trinity Sunday

YEAR C

Blessed are you, Father, Son and Holy Spirit,
Three Persons in One God.
To you be praise and glory for ever.
In your goodness you have revealed yourself to us
and invited us to share in your glory.
Blessed are you, God, for ever.

Father, we give you thanks for your creation,
for the beauty and wonder of our world.
We ask your blessing upon all who work in caring for the earth
and who labour to provide us with our daily needs.
May your Church lead others
to respect the world and each other.
We ask your blessing upon family life
and upon all relationships.

Silence

Holy, holy, holy God,
hear us and help us.

Jesus Christ, Son of God, we give thanks
for your love revealed in our salvation.
May we share with you
in the bringing of all people to a greater freedom.
We pray for the emergency services
and for all who risk their lives on behalf of others.
We ask your blessing upon all who are caring
for the ill and hungry of our world.

Silence

Holy, holy, holy God,
hear us and help us.

Holy Spirit of God, may we know your presence
with us and within us.
We give thanks for the talents and the abilities you give to us.
We pray for all scientists and research workers,
for all artists and craftspeople.
We ask your blessing upon all who teach
and those who learn.

Silence

Holy, holy, holy God,
hear us and help us.

Holy and blessed Three,
we wonder at your unity and diversity.
We pray for our families and our homes.
We remember before you
all who are having difficulties in their relationships
and all who suffer from mental illness or autism.
We pray for all who are separated from loved ones
through illness.

Silence

Holy, holy, holy God,
hear us and help us.

You, Lord, are our Creator, Redeemer and Guide.
As you have made us and redeemed us,
you offer us new life and life eternal.
We remember in your presence
all our loved ones and friends who are departed from us.
May they rejoice in your love and presence
now and for evermore.

Silence

Merciful Father,
accept these prayers
for the sake of your Son,
our Saviour Jesus Christ.
Amen.

Proper 4

Sunday between 29 May and 4 June inclusive
(if after Trinity Sunday)

YEAR C

Blessed are you, Father, Son and Holy Spirit.
You hear our prayers and are ever ready to help us.
May we live in awareness of your presence and your peace
and rejoice in your abiding love and in your power.
Blessed are you, one God for ever.

We give thanks for all who have sustained us
through their prayers,
who have interceded on our behalf.
We ask you to bless all who exercise a ministry of intercession.
We pray for religious communities.
We ask you to guide all who are concerned
with the outreach and mission of the Church
and we ask for your blessing
upon the outreach of our church to the local community.

Silence

Lord of all power,
hear us and help us.

We give thanks for all who are involved
in communication and education.
We pray for schools, colleges and universities,
those who teach and all who are learning new things.
We ask your blessing upon those involved
with broadcasting and the press.
We pray for freedom of the press
and freedom of speech for all peoples.

Silence

Lord of all power,
hear us and help us.

We give thanks for those who have given us of their love,
who have spent time and their lives in caring for us.
We ask your blessing upon our homes and all whom we love.
We pray for homes where there is little love
and poor communication.

Silence

Lord of all power,
hear us and help us.

We give thanks for our lives and all who have enriched them.
We pray for all who suffer from autism
or have problems communicating.
We remember those who suffer from deafness
or the inability to speak.
We pray for those who are suffering from Alzheimer's disease
and all who are too frail or ill to look after themselves.

Silence

Lord of all power,
hear us and help us.

We give thanks for the communion of saints
and rejoice that we have a share with them in your kingdom.
We remember before you our friends and loved ones
who are departed from us.
May they rest in peace and rejoice in glory.

Silence

Merciful Father,
accept these prayers
for the sake of your Son,
our Saviour Jesus Christ.
Amen.

Proper 5

Sunday between 5 and 11 June inclusive
(if after Trinity Sunday)

YEAR C

Blessed are you, Father, Son and Holy Spirit.
You have created light and life
and you offer to us your light and your life.
In you we triumph over death
and are given the gift of eternal life.
Blessed are you, one God for ever and ever.

We give thanks to you, O Father,
that in Jesus is the resurrection and the life,
and that through him we have the victory over death.
We give thanks for the Good News of the Gospel
and pray for all who seek to proclaim your love and salvation.
We ask your blessing on all who preach the word
and who administer the sacraments.
We pray especially for those who are working
with the under-privileged and marginalised of the world.

Silence

Strong and saving God,
hear us and help us.

We give thanks for our lives
and we remember before you
all who suffer from poverty, from war or from prejudice.
We ask your blessing upon all homeless people
and all who are out of work.
We pray for those who are unable to cope
with their circumstances
and whose lives are spiralling out of control.

Silence

Strong and saving God,
hear us and help us.

We remember before you our homes and our loved ones.
We ask your blessing upon our families and friends.
We pray especially for homes where there is illness or poverty
and any home where there has been a recent death.

Silence

Strong and saving God,
hear us and help us.

We rejoice in the gift of life
and ask that you will protect us and help us at all times.
We pray for all who are suffering from a debilitating illness.
We remember those who are suffering from blindness
and all who through illness can no longer work.
We pray for loved ones who are separated through illness
and for all who are in a hospice at this time.

Silence

Strong and saving God,
hear us and help us.

We ask your blessing
upon our loved ones who have departed this life,
that they may live with you and know your peace.
We rejoice in the gift of eternal life
and in the fellowship of all your saints.
May we share with them
in the fullness of your kingdom in glory.

Silence

Merciful Father,
accept these prayers
for the sake of your Son,
our Saviour Jesus Christ.
Amen.

Proper 6

Sunday between 12 and 18 June inclusive
(if after Trinity Sunday)

YEAR C

Blessed are you, Father, Son and Holy Spirit,
for you welcome us into your presence.
You forgive our sins and give us the power,
through contact with you, to walk in newness of life.
In your love you accept us and offer us eternal life.
Blessed are you for ever.

We give thanks for all who have come to know
the joy of your forgiveness
through the ministry of your Church.
Help us to know that, though you do not love the sin,
you do love and accept the sinner.
We pray for all who share in healing and forgiveness.
We ask you to bless all who care for others,
all who preach the word, those who administer the sacraments
and those who counsel any who are in trouble.

Silence

Lord, we come to you:
hear us and help us.

We give thanks for your forgiveness
and we pray for all who are consumed
by guilt and bad memories.
We pray for all who are unable to forgive others or themselves.
We remember all who are surrounded by self-righteousness
and feelings of self-sufficiency.
We ask your blessing on all who find it hard
to make contact with others,
all who are lonely and all who feel unwanted.

Silence

Lord, we come to you:
hear us and help us.

We give thanks for all who have shown us love and forgiveness,
for those who loved us even when we hurt them by our actions.
We pray for all who love us and share our lives.
We remember friends and loved ones
with whom we have lost contact.
We pray for all who suffer from relationships
that are broken by past sins
and cannot find healing.

Silence

Lord, we come to you:
hear us and help us.

We pray for all who are ill or suffering at this time.
We ask your blessing upon all who suffer
through the sin and violence of others.
We pray for all who are caught up
in vice, drugs and addiction.
We ask for your healing upon our society and our lives.

Silence

Lord, we come to you:
hear us and help us.

As we affirm the forgiveness of sins
and the resurrection of the body,
we pray for our friends and loved ones
who are departed from us.
May they know the joy of your forgiveness
and rejoice with your saints in life eternal.

Silence

Merciful Father,
accept these prayers
for the sake of your Son,
our Saviour Jesus Christ.
Amen.

Proper 7

Sunday between 19 and 25 June inclusive
(if after Trinity Sunday)

YEAR C

Blessed are you, Lord our God,
for you created order out of chaos
and the world out of your love.
You offer peace and well-being to all of your creation.
Blessed are you, Father, Son and Holy Spirit.

We give thanks to you, O Lord,
for all who help to bring healing and peace to your world.
May the Church be seen as an instrument
of your peace and of your love for all peoples.
May all who are distressed and disturbed
come to know the peace of Christ and his love.
We ask your blessing upon all meditation groups
and all who help others to live in harmony.

Silence

Christ, our Lord,
grant us your peace.

We pray for peace in the world:
peace between nations,
peace within all communities,
peace in our hearts and in our lives.
Lord, show us the peace we should accept,
the peace we should give,
the peace we need to work for
and the peace we should forgo.

Silence

Christ, our Lord,
grant us your peace.

We ask your blessing upon our homes,
that they may be full of your love
and that we may live in harmony with each other.
We pray for families suffering
from broken relationships or violence,
and for those who just cannot cope with life.

Silence

Christ, our Lord,
grant us your peace.

We remember all who are suffering from mental stress,
all who are experiencing a breakdown
of their lives or their personalities.
We pray for those taken into care
and those who are a danger to themselves or others.
We ask your blessing upon those
who are suffering from mental anguish or trauma.
We pray for all who are seeking to restore
health and peace to individuals or communities.

Silence

Christ, our Lord,
grant us your peace.

We rejoice in the peace that passes all understanding
and pray that our loved ones departed
may know the peace and joy of eternal life.

Silence

Merciful Father,
accept these prayers
for the sake of your Son,
our Saviour Jesus Christ.
Amen.

Proper 8

Sunday between 26 June and 2 July inclusive

YEAR C

Blessed are you, Father, Son and Holy Spirit.
You have called us into life.
You call each of us to reveal your presence and your love.
Make us worthy of our calling
and help us to do what you would have us do.
To you be glory and blessing for ever and ever.

Lord God, may we heed your voice
and obey your commands,
that we may witness to you and your saving power.
We pray that all within your Church
may be enabled to fulfil their vocation.
We remember all who are seeking to serve you
through their baptism, confirmation or ordination.
We pray that your Church may grow
in outreach and in number.
We ask your blessing upon all who are called
to be prophets or priests at this time.

Silence

Lord, you have created us:
make us worthy of our calling.

We give thanks for all who seek to serve others.
We pray for our Queen and for all who are in government.
We ask your blessing upon the work of the United Nations
and all who are striving to bring peace to our world.
We remember those who are working with refugees
and the poor of the world.

Silence

Lord, you have created us:
make us worthy of our calling.

We give thanks for those who have helped us
to develop our talents and abilities.
We pray for our homes and for those who have taught us.
Bless all schools, colleges and universities.
May our homes reflect your grace and goodness,
your love and your acceptance of the needy.

Silence

Lord, you have created us:
make us worthy of our calling.

We give thanks for our freedom
and we pray for all who feel frustrated
and who feel their vocation has been thwarted
through illness, poverty or oppression.
May they know that God always has a calling for us –
even when our first calling is not possible.
We pray for all who are suffering at this time
and ask your blessing upon all who are called
to care for the ill and the lonely.

Silence

Lord, you have created us:
make us worthy of our calling.

We give thanks that you call us to eternal life
and to the joy of your presence in your kingdom.
We rejoice in the fellowship of your saints
and pray for our loved ones departed.
May we all enjoy serving you now and for ever.

Silence

Merciful Father,
accept these prayers
for the sake of your Son,
our Saviour Jesus Christ.
Amen.

Proper 9

Sunday between 3 and 9 July inclusive

YEAR C

Blessed are you, Lord our God,
for you reach out to each of us
in love and in peace.
You offer us your healing and power
and you call us to share in telling this Good News
to all people.
Blessed are you, Father, Son and Holy Spirit.

We give thanks to you, O Lord,
for the good news of the Gospel.
We ask your blessing upon all who seek
to share in the mission and outreach of Christ.
May the Church grow in holiness,
in outreach and in number.
We pray for missionary societies
and for all who are seeking to spread the good news.
Grant that we may share in this mission.

Silence

Lord of the harvest,
may your kingdom come in us.

We pray for those who harvest the crops of the world.
May no one suffer from the greed and selfishness of others.
We pray that the hungry may be fed
and all refugees and homeless people cared for.
We ask you to guide those who are in charge
of multinational companies,
that their labourers may get fair wages and justice.

Silence

Lord of the harvest,
may your kingdom come in us.

We give thanks for those who have taught us the faith
and shared their love of God.
We ask your blessing upon our homes and our friends.
We pray for those of our friends
who do not know you and have not heard the Gospel.

Silence

Lord of the harvest,
may your kingdom come in us.

We ask your blessing upon the hungry of the world,
those who are without food
and those hungry for the word of God.
We pray for all who are ill
and for those who have lost their employment through illness.
We remember all who are lonely
and all who are in need in any way.

Silence

Lord of the harvest,
may your kingdom come in us.

We give thanks that you offer us eternal life in Christ Jesus.
We rejoice in the fellowship of all your saints.
Bless our loved ones and friends who have departed from us.
May they enjoy the fullness and peace of your kingdom.

Silence

Merciful Father,
accept these prayers
for the sake of your Son,
our Saviour Jesus Christ.
Amen.

Proper 10

Sunday between 10 and 16 July inclusive

YEAR C

Blessed are you, Lord our God.
You come to us in our need.
You bind up our wounds and restore us to life.
May we be good neighbours to all who are in need or distress
and so share in your saving love.
Blessed are you, Father, Son and Holy Spirit.

Lord God,
as you have called us to work with you,
show us the ways of your salvation.
May your Church care for the weak and defenceless,
for the needy and the poor.
Let us never avoid our responsibility and pass by
on the other side.
We pray for the work of the Samaritans
and for all relief organisations.

Silence

Show us your ways, O Lord,
and teach us your paths.

We pray for peace and justice in our world.
We ask your blessing upon all who have suffered
from the violence and robbery of others.
We remember those who have been driven off their land
or out of their homes
by the greed of multi-national companies or of governments.
We pray for all displaced persons
and all who feel injured by others.

Silence

Show us your ways, O Lord,
and teach us your paths.

We give thanks for all who have cared for us
and who have given us support and comfort in our needs.
We ask your blessing upon our loved ones
and our neighbours.
We pray for all who seek to build up
a spirit of community within our area.

Silence

Show us your ways, O Lord,
and teach us your paths.

We give thanks for all who work in the rescue services.
We ask your blessing upon the ambulance and fire services.
We pray for social workers and carers,
for all doctors and nurses.
We remember those who quietly work
within their community
seeing to neighbours and meeting their needs.

Silence

Show us your ways, O Lord,
and teach us your paths.

We give thanks that you rescue us from death
and offer us your peace and your joy.
We remember friends and loved ones
who are departed from us
and ask that they might enjoy a closer fellowship with you
in your kingdom of peace.

Silence

Merciful Father,
accept these prayers
for the sake of your Son,
our Saviour Jesus Christ.
Amen.

Proper 11

Sunday between 17 and 23 July inclusive

YEAR C

Blessed are you, Lord our God.
You have given us the power of communication:
eyes to see, ears to hear and lips to speak.
Teach us to be attentive to your word
and to all who come to us each day.
Blessed are you, Father, Son and Holy Spirit.

We give thanks for the stillness of the church
and that you speak to us through the silence.
We pray for all who wait upon your word and seek to do your will.
We pray for all pastors and counsellors
and all who are called to listen to the needs of others.
We pray for religious communities
and for all who wait upon you in silence.

Silence

Holy and Mighty One,
hear us and help us.

Guide all our leaders in the ways of justice and of peace.
Keep our ears open to the cry of the poor and the oppressed.
We pray for the work of Christian Aid
and all who seek to feed the hungry.

Silence

Holy and Mighty One,
hear us and help us.

Lord, teach us to be sensitive to each other.
May we give time and attention where it is needed.
We ask your blessing of peace upon our homes
and all who are dear to us.

Silence

Holy and Mighty One,
hear us and help us.

We pray today for all who are anxious and over-worked,
all who are world-weary or deeply troubled.
We remember especially
any who feel the lack of love or attention,
those who feel neglected or unwanted.
We ask your blessing upon all who are ill
and those who have been taken into care.

Silence

Holy and Mighty One,
hear us and help us.

Lord, we give thanks that you attend to our needs
and care for us through to eternity.
We ask you to bless our friends and loved ones
who are departed from this life
and now rejoice in the fullness of your kingdom.

Silence

Merciful Father,
accept these prayers
for the sake of your Son,
our Saviour Jesus Christ.
Amen.

Proper 12

Sunday between 24 and 30 July inclusive

YEAR C

Blessed are you, God and Father of us all.
You created us out of your love
and redeemed us by your love.
We rejoice that you sustain us with your love
and that you never leave us.
We seek to know your presence
and to give our love to you.
Blessed are you, God, for ever.

As we rejoice in your love for all people,
may your Church strive for justice and freedom for all.
We remember all who are persecuted for their faith
and all who are oppressed by tyranny.
We ask your blessing upon all who witness
to the power of prayer and knowing you.
We pray for religious communities
and for all who preach the word
and administer the sacraments.

Silence

Father, your kingdom come in us
as it is in heaven.

As we pray for our daily needs,
we remember all who suffer
from poverty, hunger and homelessness.
We remember those who are deeply in debt
and all who are struggling to cope with life.
We ask your blessing upon all who are not sure
where their next meal will come from.
We pray for the harvests of the world and for fair trade.

Silence

Father, your kingdom come in us
as it is in heaven.

We give thanks for all who have cared for us
and supplied our needs.
We ask your blessing upon our homes and our loved ones.
We pray for all who are responsible
for upholding high standards and integrity
within our communities
and we ask that we may be an example to others.

Silence

Father, your kingdom come in us
as it is in heaven.

We give thanks for your forgiveness
and we pray for all who are burdened with guilt and remorse
and who are striving to live a new life.
We remember all who are ill at home or in hospital.
We ask your blessing upon them
and upon those who care for them.

Silence

Father, your kingdom come in us
as it is in heaven.

We trust in your never-failing love
and commend to you our friends and loved ones departed.
May they rejoice in the fullness of your kingdom,
in the joy and peace of life eternal.

Silence

Merciful Father,
accept these prayers
for the sake of your Son,
our Saviour Jesus Christ.
Amen.

Proper 13

Sunday between 31 July and 6 August inclusive

YEAR C

Blessed are you, Lord God of all creation,
for all things come from you.
You give us life.
You give us love.
You give us a world of plenty,
that we may learn to share with our neighbour
and give generously to each other as you give to us.
Blessed are you, Father, Son and Holy Spirit.

Lord, as you have called us to serve you,
make us worthy of our calling.
Teach us to be generous and caring to all who are in need,
knowing that in giving we are enriched.
May your Church be a good steward of its gifts
and reach out to where it can use its talents.
We pray for all who give of themselves generously
in mission or in pastoral care,
all who work for little financial reward
in the service of others.

Silence

Giver of all,
teach us to share.

We ask your blessing upon all who work
for fair trade and justice in our world.
Let us all realise that life cannot be bought or sold
or measured by financial worth alone.
We pray for all who are used almost as slave labour
and for those who do not get a fair day's wage for their work.
We remember those who live in slum dwellings
or in refugee camps and all who will hunger today.

Silence

Giver of all,
teach us to share.

We give thanks for all that you have given us,
for your blessing upon our homes and families.
We give thanks for all who have taught us
and been our benefactors.
We remember homes that suffer through greed
and those who, though they have many possessions,
are poor in spirit.

Silence

Giver of all,
teach us to share.

We ask your blessing upon the weary and the war-torn,
upon the weak and those whose powers are waning.
We pray for all who are ill
and especially for those who are near to death,
asking you to bless them and their loved ones
with your presence and your peace.

Silence

Giver of all,
teach us to share.

We give thanks
for all who, though poor in the eyes of the world,
are precious in your sight.
We rejoice in the fellowship of all your saints
and we remember friends and loved ones
who are departed from us.
May we all share in your love and in your kingdom.

Silence

Merciful Father,
accept these prayers
for the sake of your Son,
our Saviour Jesus Christ.
Amen.

Proper 14

Sunday between 7 and 13 August inclusive

YEAR C

Blessed are you, Lord our God,
for you have called us to know you
and to love you.
You, Lord, are our strength and our shield,
our protector and our joy.
Blessed are you, Father, Son and Holy Spirit.

Lord, in your power
may your Church be a place of peace for the anxious
and a stronghold for all who are troubled.
We ask your blessing
upon all who are involved in pastoral work
and in caring for others.
We pray for the Church's ministry
to the outcasts and marginalised people of society.

Silence

Powerful God,
protect us and give us your peace.

We pray for our world
where there are always wars and rumours of wars.
Lord, grant us peace.
Show us the peace we should give
and the peace we need to forgo.
We pray for all who are struggling
against acts of violence,
against poverty and against hunger.
We ask your blessing upon all who work for relief agencies
and upon the work of the emergency and rescue services.

Silence

Powerful God,
protect us and give us your peace.

We give thanks for the peace and security of our homes.
We ask your blessing upon our families and friends.
We pray for homes where there is neglect or abuse.
We remember all who are afraid
and unable to speak out about their troubles.

Silence

Powerful God,
protect us and give us your peace.

We rejoice in your abiding presence
and pray for all who feel lonely or anxious at this time.
We remember all who are fearful of the future
and those who are terminally ill.
We pray for those who await a doctor's diagnosis
or who are preparing to go into hospital.
We ask your blessing upon all who suffer
and upon those who care for them.

Silence

Powerful God,
protect us and give us your peace.

Lord, all our hope is in you
for you are the giver of life and life eternal.
Bless our loved ones who are departed from us.
May they share with your saints
in the glory of your kingdom.

Silence

Merciful Father,
accept these prayers
for the sake of your Son,
our Saviour Jesus Christ.
Amen.

Proper 15

Sunday between 14 and 20 August inclusive

YEAR C

Blessed are you, Lord our God,
for you have called us to share
in the inheritance of your saints in light.
You give us strength and support for our journey.
Let us look to you
who are the Lord and Creator of all.
Blessed are you, Father, Son and Holy Spirit.

O Lord our God, among the many distractions
and temptations of the world
keep our eyes and our hearts fixed on you.
As you have called us,
make us worthy of our calling,
that we may be the people you want us to be.
We pray for all who are seeking
to share in the outreach of your love
and in the proclaiming of the Gospel.
We pray today for those who publish Bibles
and make them available in different languages.

Silence

Holy and Strong One,
help us to keep our eyes fixed on you.

We remember today
all who are involved in commerce and trade.
May they seek justice and fairness in all their dealings.
We ask your blessing
upon all involved in the leisure industry.
We pray for all who are training as athletes
or who are dedicating themselves
to some form of daily routine and discipline.

Silence

Holy and Strong One,
help us to keep our eyes fixed on you.

We give thanks for our homes and loved ones
and for all who have shared their vision of life with us.
We pray for families and individuals
who seem to have lost their way
and who feel life has no meaning or purpose.

Silence

Holy and Strong One,
help us to keep our eyes fixed on you.

We remember before you
all who are exhausted or world-weary.
We pray for those who have lost sight
of where they belong or where they are going.
We pray for all lonely and marginalised people.
We ask your blessing
upon all who are ill and suffering at this time.

Silence

Holy and Strong One,
help us to keep our eyes fixed on you.

Lord, we look to you for life and life eternal.
We pray for our friends and loved ones departed
and ask that they may share with your saints
in glory everlasting.

Silence

Merciful Father,
accept these prayers
for the sake of your Son,
our Saviour Jesus Christ.
Amen.

Proper 16

Sunday between 21 and 27 August inclusive

YEAR C

Blessed are you, Lord our God,
for you sent your Son to set us free
from sin and death.
You offer us the glorious liberty
of the children of God.
Help us to reveal your love and your freedom
in the way we live and deal with each other.
Blessed are you Father, Son and Holy Spirit.

We give thanks for all who have found newness of life
and the power to start again in Christ Jesus.
We ask that our church may be welcoming
and friendly to newcomers
and invite them to share in our fellowship.
We pray for the work of prison and hospital chaplains.
We ask your blessing
upon all that are seeking to be faithful to your word,
especially any who are being persecuted for their faith.

Silence

Lord, forgive our sins
and heal our infirmities.

We give thanks for all works of renewal and restoration.
We pray for reconciliation units
and for all who seek to bring peace
to families, communities or to the world.
We pray for those who work
in the rehabilitation of drug abusers or prisoners.
We ask your blessing
upon all who work for freedom and justice in our world.

Silence

Lord, forgive our sins
and heal our infirmities.

We give thanks for the community to which we belong
and for all who maintain its well-being.
We pray for local councils
and organisations that help to enhance our world.
We ask your blessing upon our families and friends.

Silence

Lord, forgive our sins
and heal our infirmities.

We pray for all who have lost their freedom
through tyranny or war.
We remember all political prisoners
and all who are in refugee camps.
We pray for all who are prisoners due to vice or drugs.
We ask your blessing upon all who suffer
from a physical or mental handicap.
We pray for all who are housebound or in hospital.

Silence

Lord, forgive our sins
and heal our infirmities.

We rejoice in the fellowship of all your saints.
We commend ourselves and our loved ones departed
to your love
and look forward to the freedom of your eternal kingdom.

Silence

Merciful Father,
accept these prayers
for the sake of your Son,
our Saviour Jesus Christ.
Amen.

Proper 17

Sunday between 28 August and 3 September inclusive

YEAR C

Blessed are you, Lord our God,
for you come to us in love and with blessings.
You are to be met in our encounters
with friends and with strangers
as you are in all and about all.
Blessed are you, Father, Son and Holy Spirit.

We give thanks that you have called us to know you
and ask that we may always serve you faithfully.
Bless all who are called to preach the word
and administer the sacraments.
We pray for all who are training for ministry
and all who are seeking to understand and proclaim your word.

Silence

Lord God Almighty,
hear us and help us.

We pray for peace in our world.
We remember all who work for the reconciliation
of relationships in nations and in individuals.
We pray for the United Nations and all peacekeeping forces.

Silence

Lord God Almighty,
hear us and help us.

We give thanks for all who have shared their lives with us.
We pray for our homes and our loved ones.
We remember all who spend their lives in caring for others
and we ask your blessing upon all who work as hoteliers
and who offer accommodation to others.
We pray for the work of Shelter.

Silence

Lord God Almighty,
hear us and help us.

We give thanks for all who work in the healing ministry
and we pray for doctors and nurses.
We ask your blessing
upon ambulance workers and upon carers.
We remember before you friends and loved ones who are ill.
We pray especially for those
who are no longer able to look after themselves.

Silence

Lord God Almighty,
hear us and help us.

We give thanks for the gift of eternal life
and ask that your blessing be upon our friends
and loved ones who are departed from us.
May we come to share with them,
in the fellowship of all your saints,
in your glory that is for ever.

Silence

Merciful Father,
accept these prayers
for the sake of your Son,
our Saviour Jesus Christ.
Amen.

Proper 18

Sunday between 4 and 10 September inclusive

YEAR C

Blessed are you, Lord our God,
for you have created us and redeemed us;
you are ever ready to refresh and restore us.
By you we are renewed and given the power to start again.
Blessed are you, Father, Son and Holy Spirit,
One God for ever and ever.

We come as a Church broken by divisions and factions
and seek your healing.
Sometimes we have broken faith with you and with each other.
We pray for all who strive to bring unity to the Church.
We ask your blessing upon churches
that are faced with violent opposition.

Silence

Lord, we come to you:
only you can make us whole.

We ask that we may be used as instruments of peace.
We ask your blessing upon all who seek to heal the troubles
between nations and peoples.
We ask your blessing upon the work of the United Nations.

Silence

Lord, we come to you:
only you can make us whole.

We give thanks for our homes and our loved ones.
We pray for families that are suffering
from broken relationships.
We pray for all those with broken hopes
and broken dreams.

Silence

Lord, we come to you:
only you can make us whole.

We give thanks that you are our strength and salvation.
We remember all who are broken by illness.
We pray for those struggling with a nervous breakdown
and all who feel their lives are on the edge of collapse.
We ask your blessing upon all
who are no longer able to care for themselves.

Silence

Lord, we come to you:
only you can make us whole.

Lord, you make all things new
and you are the giver of life and life eternal.
We ask you to bless our loved ones departed from us,
that they may rejoice in the fullness of life.
We commend them and ourselves to your unfailing love.

Silence

Merciful Father,
accept these prayers
for the sake of your Son,
our Saviour Jesus Christ.
Amen.

Proper 19

Sunday between 11 and 17 September inclusive

YEAR C

Blessed are you, Lord God,
for you have called us out of darkness
into your glorious light.
You seek out and save all who are lost
and willing to turn to you.
You are our God and Saviour.
Blessed are you, Father, Son and Holy Spirit.

Lord, we thank you for those
who made us welcome within the Church.
May we always be open to all who are seeking you
and turning away from their sin.
We ask your blessing upon all who are pastors
and who care for your people.
We pray for all who are involved
in the ministry of reconciliation and of healing.

Silence

Lord, we turn to you:
hear us and help us.

We pray for all who have been led astray
and are caught up in crime or vice.
We ask your blessing upon all who are addicted to drugs.
We remember all who do not know of you or love you.
We ask you to guide and strengthen
all who work for the good of others
and all who seek to bring peace to our world.

Silence

Lord, we turn to you:
hear us and help us.

We give thanks for those who have taught us the Good News
and for all who have shared their faith with us.
Lord, help us to turn to you each day and to be faithful to you.
We ask your blessing upon all who are suffering
from broken relationships and broken homes.
We pray for our families and our friends.

Silence

Lord, we turn to you:
hear us and help us.

God, we remember all who feel lost
and whose life seems to have no purpose.
We remember all who feel they have failed in life
and all who despair at this time.
May they know your love and your saving power.
We pray for all who are ill at home or in hospital
and those who are caring for them.

Silence

Lord, we turn to you:
hear us and help us.

We rejoice that you care for each of us
and you delight in our coming to you.
We ask your blessing upon all our loved ones
who are departed this life.
May they delight in you and in your love.
We commend ourselves and all of creation
to your loving care.

Silence

Merciful Father,
accept these prayers
for the sake of your Son,
our Saviour Jesus Christ.
Amen.

Proper 20

Sunday between 18 and 24 September inclusive

YEAR C

Blessed are you, Lord our God,
for you have given us a wonderful world to live in.
You have given us life and all that we need
and much to enjoy.
We give you thanks and praise
for the beauty and wonder of creation,
for all things come from you.
Blessed are you, Father, Son and Holy Spirit.

We give thanks for all who serve you faithfully
in their daily work,
for all who seek to reveal your glory.
We pray for all involved in leading worship
and in preaching the word.
We ask your blessing upon all
who are seeking to care for your creation
by working for the relief of others
or for the conservation of nature.
May we all show respect for what you have given us.

Silence

O God, our Saviour,
help us, for the glory of your name.

We ask your blessing upon Elizabeth our queen,
upon all rulers and leaders.
We pray for our government
and all the governments of the world.
May all who are in positions of power
use their office to the benefit of others and the good of all.
We ask that the world may accept the peace that you offer us,
that all may live in harmony and none be oppressed.

Silence

O God, our Saviour,
help us, for the glory of your name.

We rejoice in the love and protection we have received
through our homes and our loved ones.
We ask your blessing
upon all who are struggling with their relationships
or who suffer from poverty or violence.
We pray for families who have been separated
by illness or circumstance.

Silence

O God, our Saviour,
help us, for the glory of your name.

We give thanks for all who do medical research
and all who work for the health and well-being of our world.
We ask your blessing upon the World Health Organisation.
We remember before you all who are in pain or distress,
all who are ill at home or in hospital,
all who suffer from neglect or from loneliness.

Silence

O God, our Saviour,
help us, for the glory of your name.

We give thanks for the gift of life
and the promise of life eternal.
We rejoice in the fellowship of all your saints
and in the faithful departed.
We commend them and ourselves to your unfailing love.

Silence

Merciful Father,
accept these prayers
for the sake of your Son,
our Saviour Jesus Christ.
Amen.

Proper 21

Sunday between 25 September and 1 October inclusive

YEAR C

Blessed are you, Lord our God,
for you have created us and supplied all we need.
You have created a world
where there is enough for everyone's need
but not for everyone's greed.
Teach us to live graciously as you are gracious to us.
Blessed are you, Father, Son and Holy Spirit.

God, we ask your blessing
upon your Church throughout the world,
that it may witness to your love and your saving power.
We remember especially where the Church is reaching out
to the extremely poor and the outcasts of society.
We ask you to guide
all who stand against injustice and oppression.
May your Church work for the liberation
of all who are used as slave labour
or who are in refugee camps.

Silence

God, we trust in you:
hear us and help us.

We give thanks for all you have given us, O Lord.
We remember before you all who are suffering
through famine, war or poverty.
We pray for all who live in shantytowns
or in impoverished dwellings.
We bring before you
all who do not have proper medical care or education.

Silence

God, we trust in you:
hear us and help us.

As we give thanks for the comfort of our homes,
we remember all who have been made homeless.
We ask your blessing upon all who are orphaned
and have no one to care for them.
We ask your blessing upon all children
who have been taken into care.

Silence

God, we trust in you:
hear us and help us.

We give thanks for our health service
and for all who attend to our well-being.
We pray for those throughout our world
who are suffering from AIDS
or from other illnesses for which there is no cure.
We remember especially families who have lost their income
through the adults of the house being ill.
We ask your blessing on friends and loved ones
who are suffering at this time.

Silence

God, we trust in you:
hear us and help us.

We give thanks for the faithful departed
and pray for our loved ones
who have entered into the fullness of life eternal.
We rejoice in the fellowship of all your saints
and pray that we may share with them
in your heavenly kingdom.

Silence

Merciful Father,
accept these prayers
for the sake of your Son,
our Saviour Jesus Christ.
Amen.

Proper 22

Sunday between 2 and 8 October inclusive

YEAR C

Blessed are you, Lord our God,
for you have created us out of your love and for your love.
You have revealed your love in Jesus Christ
and by the sending of the Spirit.
Lord, as you love us, we give our love to you.
Blessed are you, Father, Son and Holy Spirit.

Lord God our Father,
as we ask your blessing upon us,
may we and your whole Church
reveal your love to the world.
May people look upon us and know we are Christians
by our love for you and for all people.
We ask you to guide all who are our pastors;
we pray for all bishops and clergy.
Give wisdom to all who seek to bring others
to a deeper faith in you.

Silence

Father, we trust in you:
hear us and help us.

We give thanks for all who give their lives
in the service of others.
We remember all leaders of people,
members of governments and all rulers.
We pray that they may keep
the interest and love of others in their hearts.
We ask your blessing upon all
who seek to bring peace and healing to our world.

Silence

Father, we trust in you:
hear us and help us.

We give thanks for all who have loved us
and given us confidence.
We ask your blessing upon our homes
and all who are dear to us.
We pray for the community in which we live.
We remember especially
any who may be in need of help or guidance at this time.

Silence

Father, we trust in you:
hear us and help us.

We give thanks for all who work
for the healing and well-being of the world.
We pray for all who are suffering
from broken relationships and loneliness.
We ask your blessing
upon any who feel unloved and unwanted.
We remember before you all who are ill
and their loved ones as they share in their suffering.

Silence

Father, we trust in you:
hear us and help us.

We give thanks for your everlasting love
and for the gift of eternal life.
We ask your blessing upon our loved ones
who are departed from us.
May we all know we are one in you and in your love.
We rejoice in the fellowship of all your saints
and commend this world and ourselves to your unfailing love.

Silence

Merciful Father,
accept these prayers
for the sake of your Son,
our Saviour Jesus Christ.
Amen.

Proper 23

Sunday between 9 and 15 October inclusive

YEAR C

Blessed are you, Lord our God.
All that is within us blesses your holy name
for you forgive all our sins and heal all our infirmities;
you save our life from destruction
and provide us with many good things.
Blessed are you, Father, Son and Holy Spirit now and for ever.

We give thanks for your Church throughout the world
and ask that it might share in your healing
and bringing of peace.
We remember before you all priests and pastors,
spiritual healers and those who are chaplains
and carers of the terminally ill.
We pray for the Leprosy Mission
and its work throughout the world.

Silence

Lord, we give you thanks:
hear us and have mercy upon us.

We give thanks for all
who maintain good government and care of the nations.
We ask your blessing upon all leaders, rulers and politicians.
We remember the work of the World Health Organisation
and all who work to relieve the needs and suffering of others.
We pray for our own community
and ask that we may appreciate
all who work to keep it in good order.

Silence

Lord, we give you thanks:
hear us and have mercy upon us.

We give thanks for our homes and our loved ones,
for all who have helped us and taught us in life.
We ask your blessing upon our families,
our friends and all our relationships.
We pray for those who are separated from their loved ones
through illness or circumstance.

Silence

Lord, we give you thanks:
hear us and have mercy upon us.

We give thanks for our life and our health.
We remember before you
all who are suffering alone with no one to help.
We pray for those who are in isolation wards
and all who are unable
to join in the full life of the community.
We remember also those whom we know
who are in hospital at this time.
We ask your blessing
upon all who work in healing and in caring for the ill.

Silence

Lord, we give you thanks:
hear us and have mercy upon us.

We give thanks that nothing can separate us
from the love of God in Christ Jesus.
We remember our loved ones who are departed from us
and ask that they may enjoy the fullness of life eternal.
We rejoice in the fellowship of all your saints
and commend the world and ourselves
to your unfailing love.

Silence

Merciful Father,
accept these prayers
for the sake of your Son,
our Saviour Jesus Christ.
Amen.

Proper 24

Sunday between 16 and 22 October inclusive

YEAR C

Blessed are you, Lord our God.
You are always more ready to hear than we are to pray,
and to grant more than we desire or deserve.
May we rejoice in your presence
and know your abiding love.
Blessed are you, Father, Son and Holy Spirit.

We give thanks for all who proclaim the Gospel,
especially those who risk their lives
or their comfort for your sake.
We ask you to bless all who preach the word,
theology students
and those who take part in Bible study groups.
We pray for those who meet quietly together
to pray and to contemplate your presence and your love.

Silence

Lord, hear us,
mercifully hear us.

We ask you to guide all who work in the judicial system.
We pray for law courts, judges, barristers, solicitors and juries.
We ask your blessing upon all
who seek to keep law and order.
We pray for the police
and for social workers and probation officers.
We remember all who suffer from injustice
and whose voices are not heard.

Silence

Lord, hear us,
mercifully hear us.

We give thanks for all
who have shared their wisdom and learning with us.
We ask your blessing upon all who teach
and who influence the lives of others.
We pray for Sunday schools and day schools.
We pray for all who are deprived of a good education.
We ask you to bless and protect our homes and our loved ones.

Silence

Lord, hear us,
mercifully hear us.

We remember in your presence
the sorrows and needs of our world.
We pray for all who are oppressed
and those who have lost their liberty.
We ask your blessing upon all who are ill,
especially those who are unable to get proper attention.
We ask for your love and care
to be shown to all our loved ones
who are suffering in any way.

Silence

Lord, hear us,
mercifully hear us.

We give thanks that in your grace you offer us eternal life.
We rejoice in the fellowship of all the saints
and we pray for our loved ones who are departed from us.
May we all share with you
in the fullness of your kingdom.

Silence

Merciful Father,
accept these prayers
for the sake of your Son,
our Saviour Jesus Christ.
Amen.

Proper 25

Sunday between 23 and 29 October inclusive

YEAR C

Blessed are you, Lord God,
for in your grace and goodness
you have called us into life and to your love.
Though we are unworthy, you accept us and love us.
Blessed are you, Father, Son and Holy Spirit.

Father, you hear the prayers of the lowly
and accept the penitent sinner.
Help your Church to welcome
all who seek forgiveness and newness of life.
Let us show how we all share in your grace and goodness.
We pray for those who hear the confession of others
and for all who counsel those who are full of guilt and remorse.
May we all learn to trust in your love and acceptance.

Silence

Lord, hear us;
in your mercy hear us.

Father, we give thanks for your creation
and ask your blessing upon all who are working
to conserve and protect the earth.
We pray for the peoples of the earth
who have been moved out of their homes and land
through the greed and power of others.
Father, forgive us when we are insensitive to those who suffer
as a result of our desire for cheap products.
May we do all we can
to bring justice and fair trade to peoples and nations.
We pray for all who are oppressed at this time.

Silence

Lord, hear us;
in your mercy hear us.

We give thanks for our families and loved ones.
We remember how they have cared for us
even when we seemed to have failed their love.
We ask you to bless all who are suffering
from broken relationships and unforgiving hearts.
We remember all who are full of anger or resentment
and lack your love and peace.

Silence

Lord, hear us;
in your mercy hear us.

Father, we know that you love and care for us.
May we show that same love to others.
We ask your blessing upon all who are outcasts or refugees,
all who have been made homeless and have nowhere to go.
We remember all who are ill at home or in hospital
and ask that they may have courage and hope in their troubles.

Silence

Lord, hear us;
in your mercy hear us.

Father, you offer us the gift of eternal life
even though we are unworthy of you.
You welcome us into your kingdom.
We pray for our friends and loved ones
who have departed from us.
As they shared their lives on earth with us,
may they now share with you
in the fullness of eternal life.

Silence

Merciful Father,
accept these prayers
for the sake of your Son,
our Saviour Jesus Christ.
Amen.

All Saints' Day

1 November or Sunday between 30 October and 5 November inclusive

YEAR C

Blessed are you, Lord our God,
for in you and your love we share with the saints in glory.
For all the saints who have gone before us
and revealed your love,
for those in weakness who have revealed your power,
for those who challenge us by their deeds,
we give you thanks and praise.
Blessed are you, Father, Son and Holy Spirit.

We give thanks for all who have built up your Church
through their holiness, their witness and their faith in you.
We give thanks for those who have inspired us
and challenged our way of life.
Lord, grant us the power to be the people you want us to be
and to do what you want us to do.
Bless all who minister to us and teach us your holy word.
We pray for all who are being prepared
for baptism, confirmation, marriage or ordination.

Silence

Lord, make us to be numbered with your saints
in that glory which is everlasting.

As we give thanks for our faith and the world around us,
we remember all who are being persecuted for their faith.
We ask your blessing upon all who are risking their lives
to maintain peace and order in our world.
We ask you to bless and guide
all who stand up for the freedom and well-being
of the poor and the oppressed.

Silence

Lord, make us to be numbered with your saints
in that glory which is everlasting.

We give thanks for all who have revealed your love to us
through their own love.
We ask your blessing upon our homes and our loved ones.
We remember all who are quietly sacrificing
their lives and their freedom
in the care they are giving to others.
We ask you to bless all who are caring for the ill
and those who are handicapped or infirm.

Silence

Lord, make us to be numbered with your saints
in that glory which is everlasting.

We give thanks for all who have risked pain or death
to forward your kingdom.
We ask your blessing upon all who are struggling at this time,
all who are oppressed or who are in danger.
We pray for all who are ill at home or in hospital.
We remember all who are suffering because of their faith:
the scorned, the persecuted and the ignored.

Silence

Lord, make us to be numbered with your saints
in that glory which is everlasting.

We rejoice in the communion of saints,
that we are one in you and your love.
We remember those whose service on earth is done
and now rejoice with you in glory.
We ask your blessing
upon all who have been an inspiration to us
and have enriched our lives by their love
but are now departed from us.

Silence

Merciful Father,
accept these prayers
for the sake of your Son,
our Saviour Jesus Christ.
Amen.

Fourth Sunday before Advent

Sunday between 30 October and 5 November inclusive; for use if the Feast of All Saints was celebrated on 1 November and alternative propers are needed

YEAR C

Blessed are you, Lord our God,
for you love us with an everlasting love.
You sent your Son to descend into the depths of our lives,
that he may raise us up to the fullness of life eternal.
In you and in the power of your Spirit we can be changed
and have the power to live to your glory.
Blessed are you, Father, Son and Holy Spirit.

We give thanks that you seek and desire to save
all who are lost or in the depths.
We ask you to guide and bless all who are new to the faith,
the newly converted, the baptised and the confirmed.
Bless, O Lord, all who are seekers
and those who are longing for a change in their lives.
We remember all who are growing in the faith
and those who have discovered a living relationship with you.

Silence

Lord, you seek and save the lost:
hear us as we call upon you.

We ask your guidance
upon all who are involved in commerce and in high finance,
upon tax collectors, workers in the stock market and bankers.
We remember all who are involved
with the International Monetary Fund.
We ask your blessing upon countries that are deeply in debt
and upon the poor of the world.
We pray for all who are spiritually or materially bankrupt.

Silence

Lord, you seek and save the lost:
hear us as we call upon you.

We give thanks to you for our homes
and all that you have given us.
May we learn to share with those around us
and to be aware of the needs of others.
We remember all who have lost their homes
or their employment this week
and we pray for children taken into care.

Silence

Lord, you seek and save the lost:
hear us as we call upon you.

We remember all who have lost their way
and become involved in drugs or violence,
all who are suffering through the decadence of society.
We ask your blessing upon all who are ill at home or in hospital
and all who are fearful for their future.

Silence

Lord, you seek and save the lost:
hear us as we call upon you.

We give thanks that Jesus came down
to seek us and to lift us up into your kingdom,
for the forgiveness of sins
and the opportunity to amend our lives.
We rejoice in the fellowship of all the redeemed.
We ask you to bless our loved ones who are departed from us
and are now in your nearer presence and love.

Silence

Merciful Father,
accept these prayers
for the sake of your Son,
our Saviour Jesus Christ.
Amen.

Third Sunday before Advent

Sunday between 6 and 12 November inclusive

YEAR C

Blessed are you, Lord our God,
for you give us life and life eternal.
You have given us the power to grow and to change.
You have given us the freedom to ignore or turn to you.
In your love you seek us
and want us to have the fullness of life.
Blessed are you, Father, Son and Holy Spirit.

God, we thank you for the Holy Scriptures,
for those who have preached the word
and brought the Good News to our land.
May we not be narrow-minded in our views
or fail to bring the Scriptures to bear on our experience.
We ask you to guide all who are intolerant
towards the faith of others,
that they may be more loving.
We seek your blessing upon our own clergy and ministers.
We pray for all who are struggling with their faith.

Silence

Lord, hear our cry:
listen to our prayer.

We give thanks for all we have received
and we ask that we might be generous in our sharing.
We ask your blessing upon all who are working
for justice and fair dealing.
We remember all who suffer from oppression or from poverty.
Lord, give strength to all who are working
for the freedom of others and for peace in our world.

Silence

Lord, hear our cry:
listen to our prayer.

We give thanks for the wonder of life,
for growth and for change.
We pray to you for our parents
and for those who have helped us to grow and learn.
We ask your blessing upon all who care for families
who are in trouble or in difficulty.
We pray for social services and probation workers.

Silence

Lord, hear our cry:
listen to our prayer.

We give thanks for the renewing powers of the body.
We ask your blessing upon all
who are involved in healing and in the care of the ill.
We ask you to protect and strengthen
our loved ones who are suffering at this time
and we remember before you all suffering peoples.

Silence

Lord, hear our cry:
listen to our prayer.

We give thanks for the power of the resurrection of our Lord.
Through him may we come to rejoice in eternal life.
We ask your blessing upon our loved ones
and all the faithful departed.
May they share in the joys of your kingdom.

Silence

Merciful Father,
accept these prayers
for the sake of your Son,
our Saviour Jesus Christ.
Amen.

Second Sunday before Advent

Sunday between 13 and 19 November inclusive

YEAR C

Blessed are you, Lord our God.
You never leave us or forsake us.
You are a present help in our troubles.
You are our strength and our salvation.
In you, O Lord, we trust.
Blessed are you, Father, Son and Holy Spirit.

We give thanks
for all who have shared their faith with us
and all who have witnessed to you in times of trouble.
We ask your blessing
upon all who are struggling with their faith at this time,
all who are caught up with doubt
or who are giving way to despair.
May the light and love of Christ bring them new hope.
We remember before you
all who are being persecuted for their faith.
We pray for churches that are suffering
from war, violence or vandalism.
We pray for all who have lost their place of worship.

Silence

Lord, you are our strength
and our salvation.

Lord, guide and strengthen the leaders of the world.
Give wisdom to all who rule and who are in government.
We pray for all who are involved with famine relief
or who seek to bring peace among nations.
We remember all who have been made homeless
or driven off their own land.

Silence

Lord, you are our strength
and our salvation.

We give thanks for the shelter and security of our homes.
We remember homes where it is hard to be a Christian
and where faith in you is discouraged.
We pray for children who are not given any sense of faith
or confidence in the future.
We ask your blessing upon our families
and all our loved ones.

Silence

Lord, you are our strength
and our salvation.

We remember all lonely and uncared-for people;
may they know your love and your presence.
We ask your blessing upon all who are ill
and those who fear the future.
We pray for those who are in care
and for all who cannot cope on their own.

Silence

Lord, you are our strength
and our salvation.

We give thanks to all who have witnessed
to your love even to death.
We pray for all who have died for their faith in you
and we remember the holy martyrs.
We ask your blessing upon our loved ones departed from us.
May we share with them in the joys of your eternal kingdom.

Silence

Merciful Father,
accept these prayers
for the sake of your Son,
our Saviour Jesus Christ.
Amen.

Christ the King

Sunday between 20 and 26 November inclusive

YEAR C

Blessed are you, Lord our God,
for you love us with an everlasting love
and sent your Son to be our Saviour.
He came and died that we might live.
Now he is the King of kings and Lord of lords.
May we do your will and share in your kingdom.
Blessed are you, Father, Son and Holy Spirit.

Father, we give you thanks
that in Christ Jesus you have redeemed the world.
He died that we might live.
He reigns with you and seeks us to be part of his kingdom.
We pray for all who are seeking to serve you in their daily lives.
We remember especially
any who are being persecuted for their faith.
Lord, give us the courage to speak for you
and to witness to your love.

Silence

Lord, your kingdom come
in us as in heaven.

We ask your blessing upon all leaders of people,
all governments and rulers.
We long for the time when the kingdoms of earth
will become the kingdom of Christ our Lord.
We ask you to guide and strengthen
all who work for peace and justice.
Inspire all who seek to enrich your world
through art, music or through their daily lives.

Silence

Lord, your kingdom come
in us as in heaven.

Lord Jesus, come as our King and rule in our lives.
May we seek to serve you in our homes and in our daily work.
May we strive for your kingdom in all our dealings.
We ask your blessing upon all who are dear to us;
through their love may we learn to love you more.

Silence

Lord, your kingdom come
in us as in heaven.

We remember all who have lost faith in you
or in their neighbours.
We pray for all who walk in darkness,
for the discouraged and the despairing.
May they come to know your love and saving power.
We ask your blessing upon all who are suffering
and all who are distressed at this time.
We pray especially for friends who are ill.

Silence

Lord, your kingdom come
in us as in heaven.

We give thanks for the victory of our Lord
over hatred, darkness and death,
and that he has opened the kingdom to all who turn to him.
We pray for your blessing
upon our loved ones departed from us.
May they rejoice in the fullness and glory of your kingdom.

Silence

Merciful Father,
accept these prayers
for the sake of your Son,
our Saviour Jesus Christ.
Amen.

Other David Adam books

Welcoming the Light
1501195

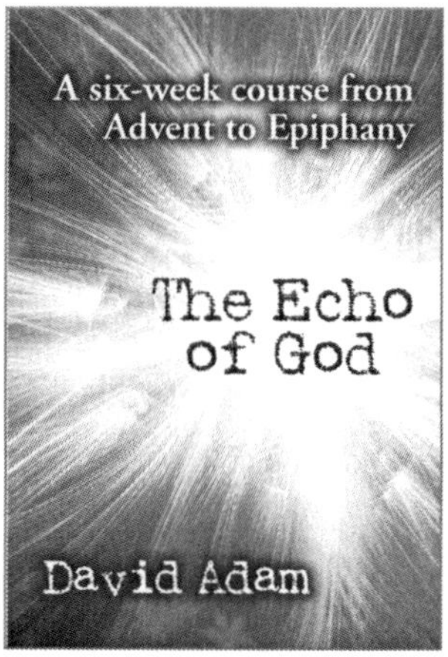

The Echo of God
1501113

Daily Prayer
1501124

A Prayer a Day
1501134